THE FIRST TIME GARDEN

THE FIRST TIME GARDEN

GEOFF HAMILTON

BBC BOOKS

PICTURE ACKNOWLEDGEMENTS

BRUCE COLEMAN/ERIC CRICHTON pages 104, 149(t),
173(tr); PHOTOS HORTICULTURAL pages 56(r), 120, 121,
145(tl), 148, 149(b), 164(t and c), 173(tl and b), 176(tr), 188(tl); HARRY
SMITH COLLECTION pages 36(b), 56(l), 57(b), 101, 144, 145(tr
and b), 164(bl and br), 176(tl and b), 188(tr); ELIZABETH
WHITING AND ASSOCIATES pages 45(t), 57(t).

All other photographs were specially taken by STEPHEN HAMILTON.

Published by BBC Books,
a division of BBC Enterprises Limited,
Woodlands, 80 Wood Lane, London W12 0TT
First published 1988
Reprinted 1988
Reprinted 1990

ISBN 0 563 20644 6 (Paperback)
0 563 20725 6 (Hardback)

Set in 10/12pt Sabon, and
Printed and bound by Butler & Tanner Ltd, Frome and London
Colour separations by Technik Litho Plates Ltd
Jacket/cover printed by Fletchers of Norwich

CONTENTS

INTRODUCTION

The most exciting thing you'll ever do in your gardening life is to create your first new garden.

Oh, certainly your initial reaction when you first look out of the window at a sea of mud liberally sprinkled with bricks, roofing tiles, bits of rusty wire, concrete bags and probably even a kitchen sink or two, will be a groan of dismay. How on earth are you ever going to turn that disaster area into a thing of beauty?

Well, that's just why we made the TV series and wrote this book. With a little bit of help, you certainly *can* do it, and once you get started, you'll enjoy every minute.

Look upon your new, expensive rubbish tip as a clean canvas and yourself as a latter-day Leonardo. You have the most marvellous opportunity to create a *masterpiece* exactly as you want it.

It all sounds rather far-fetched perhaps, at the moment, but believe me, it's not such a daft analogy as it sounds. *Everyone* can make a beautiful garden because you'll be working in close cooperation with an old master – Nature. She's made millions of gardens in her time and she'll be just as keen to make yours a success as all the others.

What's more, in just one season you'll be able to transform that bare, cluttered soil into a little bit of paradise.

You may feel that the cost is going to be beyond you. After all, some of the prices at the garden centre are – well, optimistic to say the least! And we're always hearing about how expensive gardening has become. Well, that's just so much stuff and nonsense.

Half of what you'll be pressured to buy is quite unnecessary and much can be made at home or bought slowly. There's certainly no need to break the bank or even go without the curtains or the carpets. The thing to remember is *always* to buy good quality. Buying the cheapest plants, tools or sundries is often the most expensive way in the end.

Some of the tools and equipment needed in the construction of the garden are, admittedly, expensive. What's more, you'll probably only use them when you actually build the garden. After that, they'll sit in the shed until you move to the next garden. But all this equipment can be hired at a fraction of the cost of buying it. Everything from a cold chisel to a cement mixer is available at your local tool-hire shop, so one of the first jobs should be to get hold of their price list and find out what's available. It could save you pounds.

You may be put off by the thought of all the work a good garden entails. Well, I can tell you this. A well-thought-out and properly planted garden will take half the work demanded by a weed-infested mess. Cutting a good lawn once a week, for example, takes a fifth of the time needed to cut a poor one once a month! Weeding a well-planted garden is something you'll actually look forward to doing once or twice a year. Well-grown plants in well-planned borders just won't put up with an invasion by the riff-raff!

But worst of all, you may feel that you just don't *like* gardening. Most of us have memories of all that interminable, boring weeding we had to do for Dad when we were kids, and anyway, gardening is supposed to be an old man's sport!

All I can say is – look, just give it a go. It's pretty dumb to condemn anything out of hand without giving it a good chance. That way you'll never know what you're missing. Sure, we all hated the enforced weeding sessions and I have to agree that trolling round with the mower is not the most exciting thing in the world. But take my word for it, creating a thing of beauty from scratch certainly *is* exciting and it's very rewarding indeed.

The great thing about the art of gardening design and construction is that it's not the exclusive domain of the highly talented. You may not be able to blow a trumpet, paint in oils or write a best-seller. But you *can* make a beautiful garden, because that's something we can *all* do.

When we set out to make the T V series, we decided right from the start that *realism* was essential. It was very tempting to locate it in my own garden at Barnsdale where all the facilities are to hand and where the soil has been worked to a high state of fertility. There are no kitchen sinks buried there and no manhole covers stuck four feet in the air! But no, that just wouldn't do. If you were going to have problems, we wanted them too!

So, we prevailed upon Barratt Homes to get the permission of one of their first-time buyers to let us use the garden on a new development in Birmingham. We were lucky. Not only were the new owners just about the most cooperative people we could have wished for (they rewarded the constant disruption and the sea of mud with cheery smiles and endless cups of tea!), but they were blessed with *all* the problems any new home-owner is ever likely to encounter. I won't depress you with a catalogue now, but the sad story will unfold as you read on!

In the series, we were faced with something of a dilemma. Because we wanted the garden to be typical of the kind of plot most first-time buyers are likely to get, it had to be small. With houses getting pushed closer and closer these days, the gardens are forever shrinking. Trouble is that in a tiny garden, there's no room to show alternatives.

We solved the problem by including as much as was possible in that garden and then going outside to other small gardens to see what other design-and-build teams had come up with. All the other gardens we visited were built by members of the British Association of Landscape Industries. That's the trade organisation whose high standards ensure that only the cream of the landscape industry become members. So the gardens are not only well designed, but they're built by craftsmen too.

Naturally, there were still techniques that we simply couldn't cram into the six programmes without skimping on the whole lot. So while you'll find details of all the methods we used and showed in the series, I've also described here lots of other projects you may feel you'd like to undertake but which we simply didn't have time to show.

I've tried to keep everything as simple as possible and to make the instructions clear and graphic. I hope that real first-timers will soon begin to realise that there's not as much magic and mystery about the noble art of making a garden as they first thought. And I fervently pray that 'old hands' will bear with me for giving away some of their secrets!

However much of a mess the site may look at the outset, it really is possible to create a garden within six months. *Opposite.* It seems hard to believe that this was our first sight of the plot. Not exactly designed to encourage!

PLANNING

Planning a garden is not a thing to do in a hurry. When we took our first look at the little plot we'd acquired for the *First Time Garden* series, we realised that the problems we'd taken on would take a fair bit of head-scratching to sort out. Mind you, we saw it at its worst.

I arrived with fellow presenter Gay Search one cold, wet December day to a scene of utter chaos! The road was a sea of mud, the house itself was still just a half-completed shell and the 'garden' was somewhere under an enormous pile of rubble. We wondered, when we got out of the car, about the cause of the dull thudding noise we could all hear. On enquiry, it turned out to be the sound of explosives experts blasting away the solid block of 15-foot (4.5 m) thick concrete that had once supported a factory on the site. We discovered later that it was from underneath that concrete that our new garden had been delivered. Not a promising start!

The view was not exactly inspiring either – not unless you have a liking for dilapidated nineteenth-century chemical factories! Talk about 'dark satanic mills' – this was certainly no 'rural idyll'.

We were about to seek the sanctuary of the car and go for a quick morale booster in the nearest local when we were dealt the final blow. With a screeching whistle, a roar and a rush, a hundred yards of Intercity Express flashed past the garden – no more than 20 feet from our patio doors!

'Well,' said my producer, 'you wanted a challenge!'

Now, looked at like that, I began to realise how barmy I'd been to suggest a difficult site in the first place! But what we did have here was one garden that encapsulated all the problems any unsuspecting first-timer was likely to encounter. Restricted space, terrible soil, enough builders' rubble to build the Great Wall of China, a regular, nerve-jangling noise every half-hour or so and a view of billows of acrid smoke rising from a heap of grime. We could certainly not be accused of making it easy for ourselves!

It took a long time to decide what to do. Alison Hainey, our designer, and I plodded round the plot like a couple of inmates of Wormwood Scrubs on exercise, just getting the 'feel' of the site. Then long discussions followed.

I suppose it could be argued that the planning stage of any garden is just about the most important. After all, that garden will be with you for a long time, so it's worth getting it at least near enough right first time.

Basics

The first thing to do is to decide what the garden is *for*. If you have small children, for example, you may decide that it has to be devoted exclusively to them as a play area. In that case, the design will be very different to that of a garden meant to be used as an extension of the house. Very often a young couple will look upon it as an outside room to be used mainly for relaxation. Or you may be keen on collecting plants or growing vegetables or, more likely, you'll want a combination of all these things.

It's also wise to project forward a few years and think about what the future use may be. Bear in mind that eventually a young couple, who now want the garden only for leisure, may decide to start a family. And, projecting even further, that children will grow up and won't need the play area any more. Sometimes a lot of time and expense can be saved by looking that far ahead. The stone circle feature in our design is a good example.

This is intended as a sunbathing area. It catches all the afternoon sun, so it's the warmest spot in the place. But it's also easily seen from the kitchen and living-room windows, so it would make an ideal play area for a family with very small children. Mum or Dad could keep a close eye on them from the house. So it might be an idea, in the early stages, to put a wooden edging round the circle and to fill it with sand for the kids to play. When they grow out of that, it could then be paved with stone blocks, straight on top of the sand.

Keep that final use to the forefront of your mind and then start making lists.

List number one should contain all the things that you simply can't do without. You're quite likely, for example, to need a washing line. If you have small children it's almost a certainty. Don't worry about where it will go just yet, just put it on the list. You may decide that you need somewhere to hide the dustbins, or a coal-bunker or even a tall, lockable gate to imprison little Johnny while you get on with the chores. Rack your brains and get them all down.

Then try to decide those features you *want* in the garden and make list number two. You're quite likely to decide that, since you want to use the garden as another 'room' for relaxing and entertaining, you need a paved area and a barbe-cue. Gardens aren't all hard work you know! A lawn may be considered essential if you have young children or, if you have a passion for flowers in the house, you may want a greenhouse.

Of course, this list is bound to be much too long ever to get everything in. So that's where list number three comes in. This is the 'compromise list' which is the result of honing everything down a scale or two. You may, for example, decide that a paved area and a lawn are too much of a luxury, and that one or the other must go. You may have to compromise on the greenhouse and settle for a smaller lean-to against one of the house walls, or you may kiss the vegetable plot goodbye and decide to grow a few salads in amongst the flower borders instead.

Eventually, you'll finish up with something like the real thing (though I'll guarantee you'll still have too much to fit in!) and the planning can start.

Surveying the plot
The first job is to draw a 'masterplan' of the plot, including just the bare bones – the boundaries, the position of the house and any permanent features that already exist, like established trees, for example. And to do that, you'll need an elementary knowledge of basic surveying. Sounds daunting, but it's as easy as anything really.

Of course, if your garden is exactly square or rectangular, there's no problem. Just measure the lengths of each side and the boundaries can be drawn straight onto the plan. Unfortunately, very few are. Our plot looked for all the world as if it was square, until we measured it, when it turned out to be anything but. So to place the boundaries accurately, we had to resort to a technique called 'triangulation'. The only equipment you need is a surveyor's tape, which can be hired for a few bob a week.

Start by measuring up the house. It can be assumed that the walls are straight and that all the angles are accurate right-angles, so there is no difficulty in transferring these measurements to paper.

Obviously you'll have to scale the measurements down and we found a scale of 1 to 50 most convenient. In other words, 1 cm on paper represents 50 cm on the ground. If you're working in metric measurements, this is a most convenient scale, but if, like me, you're an old-fashioned reactionary and have never got the hang of these 'foreign' ways, you may prefer to work in something like 1 inch to 5 feet. It doesn't matter at all which way you do it, so long as it's reasonably easy to work out and it fits your bit of paper! But, having been forced to work in metric because that's what Alison always uses (well, she's younger than me!), I must grudgingly admit that once you get the hang of it, it's by far the easiest!

Draw the outline of the house on the paper and then use it to get all your other measurements.

You need two fixed points to measure from and the two corners of the house are certainly the most convenient. All you do is to measure to a corner of the plot from one fixed point on the house and then to the same corner from another. Do the same thing with the other corners of the plot and you're ready to transfer the measurements to paper.

Scale down these measurements and, with a pair of compasses, draw an arc whose radius is equal to the first measurement and with the centre on one of the fixed points on the house. Draw another arc whose radius is equal to the second measurement from the other fixed point on the house, and where the arcs cross is the corner of the garden.

Repeat the process for the other corners of the garden and you can draw in the boundaries. Other existing features, like trees or outhouses etc., can be drawn in in the same way.

When you've committed all this to paper, it's best to get a piece of tracing paper and pin it over the top of your masterplan. You'll be doing a lot of scribbling, rubbing out and moving things about and this way, you can make as many mistakes as you like without losing the original plan. It's also a good idea, if you haven't got a drawing board, to tape the

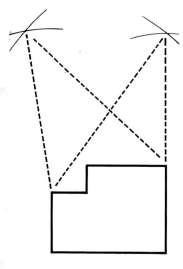

Triangulation is a simple system of measuring and marking fixed points, using the corners of the house as a 'bench mark'.

plan onto a bit of plywood or hardboard (masking tape is ideal), because you'll be referring to it regularly for at least a year and probably more.

Then you're ready to start drawing. Remember, when you do, that what you're seeing is a bird's eye view and what you'll want in the garden is a different perspective. Still, this shouldn't be allowed to worry you too much. I've found that, generally, a good, well-balanced design on paper looks good on the ground too. And, of course, you can always change the layout slightly when it comes to transferring it to the ground if it doesn't look quite right.

General principles

I don't believe there are, or should be, any hard-and-fast rules about garden design. After all, your garden is very much a personal thing and it should be made to suit you. If your neighbour doesn't like the design, well he doesn't have to look!

Quite frankly, the last thing I want to be seen as is an arbiter of 'taste', because I think that a great deal of the so-called 'fashion' in gardens and gardening is so much pre-tentious nonsense. So, please regard the following as a set of guidelines only. My observations may help you avoid making a few mistakes and so perhaps save you a little time and money, and I hope they'll start you thinking. But at the end of the day, you must do what *you* want to do!

My own first rule is to keep things simple. There's a great temptation to try to cram too much into the garden and, if it's tiny, that's a great mistake. It results only in an uncoordinated

In a small garden, it's best to keep the design simple to avoid the 'cluttered' look.

clutter with no strong focal points. It's much better to err on the side of simplicity with either straight lines or bold, sweeping curves and large expanses of materials.

It's important to think about maintenance too. If you're a busy person, a simple design will be much easier to maintain. Make sure, for example, that there are no awkward corners to mow when you design the lawn. Long, sweeping curves are not only easier but will also add to the illusion of space. Make most of the planting permanent, using trees, shrubs and herbaceous perennials which will come up every year, rather than leaving a lot of space for annuals which must be replanted each year.

Again with simplicity in mind, you should try to avoid too many different types of material in the garden. If, for example, you need a paved area and a wall, use walling blocks made of the same material as the paving or get hold of some of the same bricks used to build the house. The garden is essentially a peaceful place and my own feeling is that a jumble of different materials tends to jangle the nerves a bit!

So having determined to keep the design simple and to bear in mind the problems of maintenance, you're sitting there in front of a bare outline, wielding a sharpened pencil. What then? Where do you start?

Well, the first job is to decide on the main axis of the new garden. If you look at the plan of our plot, you'll see what I mean. Because it was so small, the garden actually appeared to be wider than it was long – a quite uncomfortable dimension. So to increase the apparent length, the axis was designed to run from corner to corner. The main viewing point would be in the corner just outside the patio doors, so the scheme is designed to draw the eye from that point to the opposite corner across the main feature – the stone circle and planted urn. Almost as soon as we decided to do that, the garden began to look twice the size!

The tricks you can play on your *perception* of space and dimension are quite surprising. If, for example, you put a striking ornament – a planted urn, a bright foliage shrub or even a statue – in one corner of the garden, the eye is automatically drawn to it. In the process, it seems to ignore what's outside the narrow tunnel of vision, making the feature look further away. If you arrange the borders so that the path to the feature – perhaps grass – narrows towards it, you create false lines of perspective and place the feature even further in the distance. Of course there are limits, but you can certainly increase the *apparent* size of the garden by careful manipulation.

It's obviously vital to take into account the position of the sun. Most of us will want to position our sitting-out area in the sunniest spot, though it might also be useful to have a cool, shady place out of the glare too. That could be especially important for retired people. When it comes to planting, obviously you'll need to put sun-lovers in an open spot and shade-lovers in the cool.

The view will be an important aspect of any garden and will inevitably prompt design decisions. If you live in beautiful countryside, you'll not want to hide stunning views; it is much better to try to incorporate the surroundings in the design. I well remember being faced with this situation in a garden I built a while ago. To make it more difficult, the plot was high up in an exposed spot, so I needed to screen it from the wind without detracting from the view.

I solved it by planting on the boundaries but leaving 'windows'. Some trees, like laburnum and the popular double-flowering cherry, have a useful habit of growth in that their branches ascend fairly steeply, rather like a triangle standing on its point. By planting two close to each other, their branches met at the top, but left a viewing hole at about eye level.

Our plot held no such delights. The view of the chemical works simply *had* to be screened, so we decided to increase the height of the fence to 9 feet (3 m) to blot the offending factory from our eyes and, we hoped, from our minds too! Of course, a 9-foot (3 m) solid fence begins to look a bit like Colditz Castle, so to avoid the claustrophobic effect we used a trellis extension. This would give a more open aspect and climbing plants would soon hide the view. And, if you really looked for it, way out on the horizon were distant views of countryside, so it would be nice to allow a peek through the foliage here and there to see that, without the ugly foreground.

Apart from the unattractive view, we also had the problem of noise from the railway line no more than a few feet away. Well, the high fence would help, but we also allowed for wide borders at that end. Massed planting really does do a very good job of damping down noise. So, we decided that the planting in front of the fence would be a mixture of trees and evergreens to give cover throughout the year.

Massed planting would have another beneficial effect. It's a strange paradox but luxuriant planting – almost overplanting

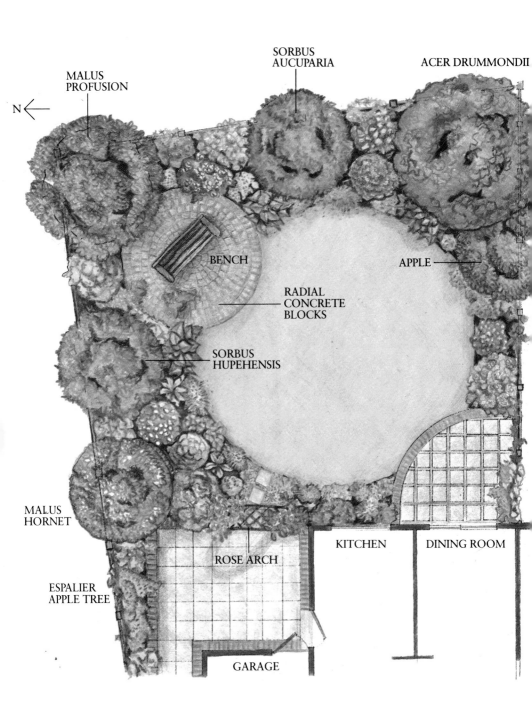

N ←

MALUS
PROFUSION

SORBUS
AUCUPARIA

ACER DRUMMONDII

BENCH

APPLE

RADIAL
CONCRETE
BLOCKS

SORBUS
HUPEHENSIS

MALUS
HORNET

KITCHEN

DINING ROOM

ROSE ARCH

ESPALIER
APPLE TREE

GARAGE

Opposite. The design for our garden in Birmingham was deliberately simple. Note that the axis runs from corner to corner to increase the apparent length.

Left. Curving the edge of the border makes lawn mowing easier, allows a greater variation of planting heights and gives a more informal appearance.

Below. Sloping sites may look daunting at first but by terracing you can create a very interesting effect.

if you like – also makes the small garden bigger. It would be logical to think that the narrower the borders and the larger the space in the middle the bigger the garden would look. But the effect of mass planting is to hide those claustrophobic fences and make it seem that your 'jungle' goes on for ever.

I visited a garden not long ago that measured just 14 feet (4 m) wide and about 30 feet (9 m) long. If you were going to swing a cat it would have to be a small one! The owner was a keen plantsman and the result was a density of planting like I'd never seen before. And that garden looked 10 times the size and was an absolute delight. It can be done.

So, make the borders a little wider than you thought you might and, instead of making them straight, vary the width by curving the edges. Not only does this give a more attractive, informal shape to them, but it also allows some wider spaces for larger plants. Thus you'll be able to vary the heights and spreads of the plants you use, resulting in a more varied and much more attractive effect.

Paths and steps are also subject to this 'optical illusion'. Wide paths make the garden look even wider while, if they are too narrow, they look cramped and mean. Mind you, once again you have to strike the happy medium. Wide paths and steps may look more noble and generous but, of course, they do take up a lot of room. And in a tiny garden, most 'proper' gardeners are going to begrudge space that could be used for plants. So you might kill two birds with one stone and use a planted stepping-stone path.

Sloping sites

These days, building land is much too valuable to waste, so you could well find your house built on a steep slope. The first reaction is to curse your luck. Yes, there certainly is going to be more work involved but, at the end of the day, you'll be much, much happier that you've inherited that slope. There's no doubt that a garden with contours is much more interesting than a perfectly flat one.

The way to cope with the slope is to terrace it into a series of plateaux, divided either by walls or banks of grass or plants. Of course, stone or brick walls will be quite expensive, but consider using railway sleepers or some of the new log-roll products that are available now. If you're in a naturally rocky area, the local rockery stone may be cheap, or you can get away with simple grass or planted banks.

When it comes to designing the terraces, try to avoid simply cutting the garden up into equal strips across from side to side. This will have the effect of foreshortening it and looks ugly. Work out a twisting path with steps at intervals and level areas of grass, paving and planting on either side.

Buildings

Most new houses these days have a garage, so a garden shed may not be absolutely necessary. If you can store your tools, machines and sundries in the garage, so much the better. But if you are misguided enough to decide that the car is more important than the mower and the spade, there are several quite attractive small buildings available that will fit in even the tiniest garden. If you have no room to hide a shed out of the way, make a feature of it by fixing wires to the outside and planting it with climbing plants.

If you can run to a greenhouse, then take the plunge and do it. Not only will it extend the gardening season right through the winter, but it will also be invaluable in raising plants. By growing all your own bedding plants and vegetable seedlings, your pot plants and cut flowers for the house plus food crops from spring to autumn, it'll very soon pay for itself.

Naturally, greenhouses should be sited in the sunniest spot and fairly near to the house if possible. That will greatly reduce the cost of putting in facilities like electricity, gas or water, and it will make those night-time trips in January to check the temperatures just a little more comfortable.

In my view, wooden greenhouses have the edge as far as looks are concerned but they do have certain disadvantages too. The big snag is that they're more expensive than aluminium and, unless you go for the astronomically priced cedar, you'll need to do a spot of painting every so often.

It's often said that aluminium is better than wood because it allows more light in. For the commercial grower who starts his tomatoes off in October and grows them right through the winter, it may be important. But for the amateur who starts sowing in February or March, when there's plenty of light for the plants to develop strongly, it's just not a factor to worry about.

If you have no room in the garden for a greenhouse, you may consider a conservatory. They're very popular these days as a means of cheaply extending the house, and they provide not only somewhere to raise plants but a place to lounge in the sun even when it's quite cold outside.

If you have room for another structure, like a pergola, a summerhouse or a rose arbour, you'll be able to provide almost instant height. Climbers will rapidly cover one of these and the garden will begin to take on an air of maturity in months rather than years.

Just one point to consider about these structures, especially if you are going to make them yourself. It's well worth asking the timber merchant for timber that has been pressure-treated with a preservative. It'll cost a little more but it more or less guarantees the wood against rotting for life.

Existing features
Sometimes, I think it's necessary to reassure new gardeners and put their minds at rest.

There is a tremendous amount of pressure these days to

conserve our natural resources and no one would deny that that's a good and necessary thing. Nonetheless, there are sometimes cases where existing plantings, and trees in particular, simply *have* to go.

If you are blessed with an enormous great sycamore in the garden that shades it out completely and allows nothing underneath but a scrappy bit of grass, then have no hesitation in getting rid of it! Well, in fact you should have just enough hesitation to check that it's not protected by a preservation order – your local council surveyor will be able to tell you that. Even if it is, you may well be able to appeal against the order and reverse it.

It's quite important to bear in mind that large, hungry trees can have a disastrous effect on the house itself. If you have a large tree like a sycamore, a poplar or a willow within about 40 feet (12 m) of the house, it could well do a lot of damage, especially if your soil is heavy. Clay soils in particular expand and contract considerably, depending on the amount of water in them. A large tree can remove an enormous amount of water in a dry spell, and this could lead to the soil under the foundations of the house contracting. Then it's possible for the footings to crack, causing serious structural damage to the house.

It's obvious, then, that if you have a tree close to your new house, it's wise to get rid of it. You should also, of course, avoid planting one! And I would go further. If you inherit trees or shrubs that are obviously much too large for the site, there is nothing wrong with pulling them out to allow you to grow more suitable subjects.

But if you do remove a tree or shrub, remember that you're morally obliged to plant another somewhere! And when you do, you'll have the opportunity of planting subjects that are more in scale with their surroundings. There is more on choice of plants later in this book.

A much knottier problem arises when the large trees shading your garden belong to your next-door neighbour. What can you do then?

Well the answer in a nutshell is, not a lot. If his trees are taking light from your house you may be able to force him to do something, but otherwise you'll just have to tailor your planting scheme to the conditions that prevail.

Opposite. This small garden is designed for a minimum of labour yet with the added interest of a pool and small greenhouse.

Of course, you are entitled to cut off branches and to sever the roots of his tree if they encroach into your garden. But there's little joy there, since a lop-sided tree presenting to your

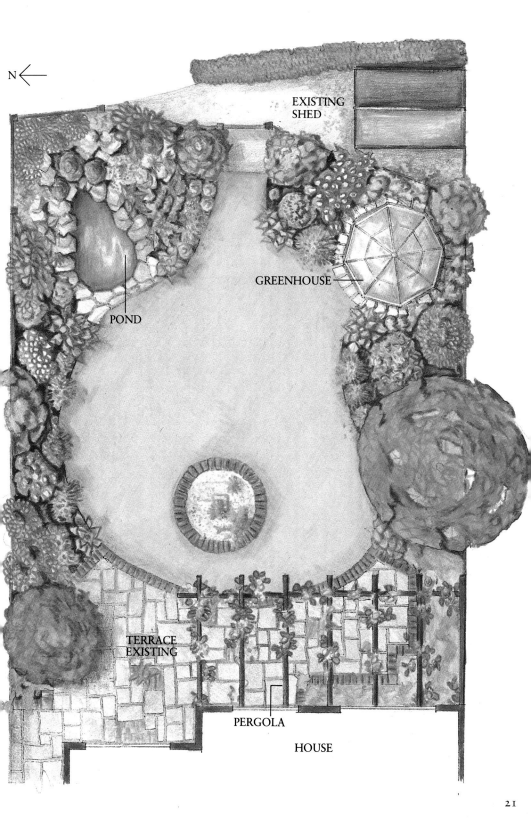

N

EXISTING
SHED

GREENHOUSE

POND

TERRACE
EXISTING

PERGOLA

HOUSE

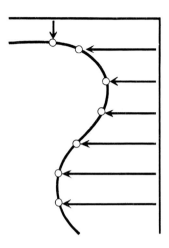

side of the garden nothing but a set of cut-off stumps is hardly an improvement. It may be worthwhile approaching your neighbour with your problem, but you can do little more. Still, you shouldn't despair, because there are plenty of marvellous plants that will thrive in shady conditions and make a great garden.

Transferring the plan

When you've finally finished the drawing and got all the discussions, arguments, disagreements and decisions out of the way, you need to preserve it with the greatest care. This is a document that's as valuable as the house deeds and has certainly taken a lot more blood, sweat and heartache to achieve. Not only will you refer to it continually during the building process but, as the first garden you've designed, it is certain to have a lot of value both in sentimental and educational terms. You'll soon discover mistakes you've made and, when you do, you'll have the plan to remind you never to commit the same error again.

If you've drawn it in pencil, it's well worth inking it in with a black pen. While you're at it, make sure you mark the centres of any circles or arcs you may have drawn. You'll be able to see them by the hole in the paper made by the compasses. When it comes to marking out the plan on the ground, those marks will be invaluable.

If possible, leave the plan on the board or re-tape it to a piece of strong cardboard and then cover the whole thing

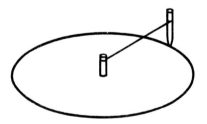

with a sheet of clear polythene stuck on with waterproof tape. That way you'll be able to take it into the garden for reference, even if your fingers are covered in mud!

Marking straight lines on the ground is, of course, fairly straightforward. Just measure from the fences and put in a garden line at the appropriate points.

Marking a circle is no more difficult provided you've remembered to mark the centre point on your plan. Simply

Marking out a circle is straightforward and obvious, using two pegs and a line. To mark curved borders, measure at intervals from the fence and use canes as markers.

measure from two fixed points to find the centre, and put in a strong cane. Then measure the radius of the circle and cut a length of string to the required length leaving enough to make a loop to slip over the cane in the centre and to tie onto a marking stick at the other end. The marking stick can then be used either to scratch a line in the soil or to put in a series of markers round the perimeter of the circle. Remember, too, to leave that centre cane in position until the very last minute, just in case you need to clarify the mark for some reason.

Marking out curves is a little more arduous. Here you should measure at fixed intervals along a straight line – perhaps the fence or the edge of a path – putting in marker canes at the appropriate distances. The drawing clearly shows the method.

Naturally, you won't need to mark out the whole garden all at once right at the start. That way you'd have so many canes in the garden it would be like a slalom obstacle course! Much better set out each feature as you come to it.

When you've done your marking out and before you actually commit yourself, take a long, hard look at the line from all angles. Bear in mind that you are viewing it from a different angle now, so it might well need adjusting a little. Since garden design is essentially a visual art, the golden rule of landscaping is that 'if it *looks* right, it *is* right'.

The plan for our garden

Our Birmingham garden was faced with just the kind of problems encountered in most modern estate houses. It was small – 38 ft × 35 ft (12 m × 11 m) – it was square and it was surrounded by high fences. In other words, it was just like living in a matchbox! The bare site looked *awful*, but a glance at the plan shows how attractive it will look in a few years' time.

The first decision was to swing the axis of the garden so that, instead of looking from front to back, the eye was taken from corner to corner. That increases the apparent length at a stroke. The main viewing point would be from the small quadrant of paving outside the dining-room doors, so the circular feature was planned to entice the viewer to look across to it. An attractive tree at the back added to the effect.

Taking away the square look is achieved in two ways. First of all, there is a circular motif, repeated in the quadrant of paving, the lawn and then the paved feature. This also allows for a good variation in the width of the borders and plenty

A difficult small garden on a slope. The problem has been cheaply and effectively solved by using wooden stakes to retain the soil, creating a series of terraces. In addition, an informal flight of steps has been made using logs as risers, with pounded soil covered with shredded bark as the treads.

HEDGE

COMPOST

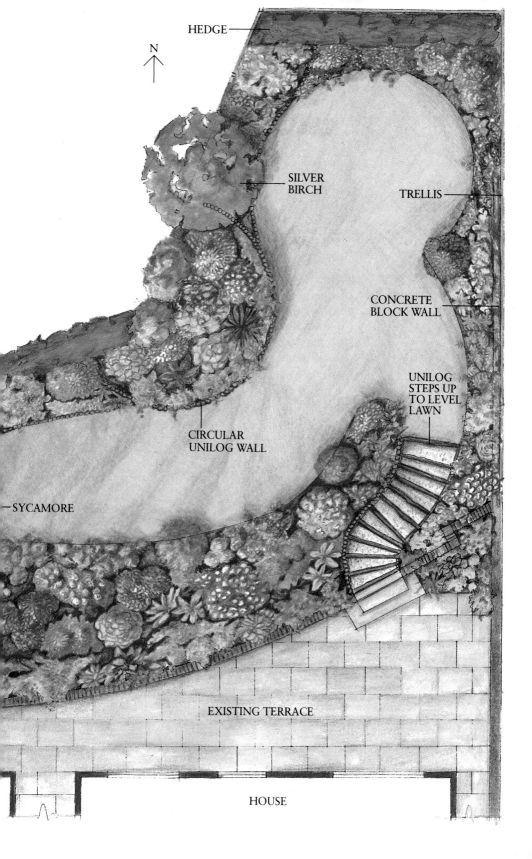

HEDGE

N

SILVER
BIRCH

TRELLIS

CONCRETE
BLOCK WALL

UNILOG
STEPS UP
TO LEVEL
LAWN

CIRCULAR
UNILOG WALL

SYCAMORE

EXISTING TERRACE

HOUSE

of room for some tall plants in the back. Combined with the climbers on the fences, this will completely obscure the preponderance of woodwork which seemed so overpowering before any planting was done. It will also, of course, effectively reduce the noise of the trains running just behind the back fence.

Note that the materials have been kept as uniform as possible. It's a mistake to mix them too much in a small garden, so the paving used outside the dining-room doors is the same as that in the utility area and the same paving blocks used to make the circular feature have been introduced to edge the paved quadrant. Because the next-door garden was on a higher level, we were forced to build a retaining wall at the edge of the utility area. To avoid using yet another material, we bought a few bricks from the builders so that they matched the house.

The planting is fairly simple. We used only plants that are freely available at the garden centre, but we made quite sure each one would work for its living by providing a display over as long a period as possible.

A separate vegetable and fruit garden was really impossible in the space, so we have contented ourselves with mostly trained fruit on the fences and vegetables mixed in with the flowers. It works very well.

Obviously it's impossible to include all the features we would have liked. The garden is just too small. So to give you a taste of other planners' ideas, we visited a couple of gardens that had been designed by professional designers. If you feel you simply can't face doing it yourself, this is, of course, a way out. Many good garden centres employ landscape architects who will either visit your site and then provide a plan or, a little cheaper, will work from your rough drawings and photographs. Most gardening magazines offer this service too.

A small plot

This garden was much the same size as ours – 40 ft × 29 ft (12 m × 9 m) – and just as square. In fact the main principles of the design are much the same. Again the designer has looked to curved paving and lawn to reduce the squareness of the plot and he too has restricted the hard materials to brick and paving slabs. Note the use of the brick edging around the central bed and the edge of the paved area, and the inclusion of the same bricks in the random paving pattern.

He has added interest by including a pool made with a plastic liner. It is informal in design and this has permitted the inclusion of a couple of rock outcrops that can be planted with alpine plants, which goes some way towards satisfying his client's passion for plants.

The small greenhouse is also a clue to an interested gardener. The octagonal shape is ideally suited to a small plot because it can be sited almost anywhere without looking out of place.

Again the fences have been covered with climbers, and further provision for some upward planting has been provided by the wooden pergola over the patio.

The circular bed in the centre of the lawn is gravelled and planted with alpine plants – a clever way to disguise a very obtrusive manhole cover.

A problem garden

Now here was a real headache. This is a garden ideally suited to a gardener with one leg considerably longer than the other! Before grading work started, the slope in one place was almost vertical and nowhere was there a level spot. It's also a very peculiar shape and measures 58 ft × 66 ft (18 m × 20 m) down the straight sides.

Obviously there was a lot of terracing to do and a lot of steps to build. To have done it all in stone or brick would not only have looked overpoweringly hard but it would have greatly exceeded the budget too.

The solution was to make the whole garden very informal. So the retaining walls have been made with lengths of logs driven into the bank and very firmly secured. The steps are made with the same material infilled with gravel. It's a cheap and very effective answer to a difficult problem.

Retaining the soil and actually increasing the slope of the banks in places has made it possible to provide at least an area of level lawn and a paved patio. So the garden can be used as well as looked at.

Because of the difficulty in cultivating the steep banks, most of them have been planted with low-maintenance shrubs underplanted with ground cover. Eventually there will be very little work to do, and it will always be a garden that can be enjoyed.

STARTING WORK

With the plan committed to paper, the real work can now begin. It'll be a relief to get rid of some of that rubbish.

Generally most of it can be put into plastic bags and carted down to the tip in the boot of the car. If you've been unlucky enough to be landed with all the builders' rubble from the whole estate, you may well need a skip. They can be hired by the day reasonably cheaply but, before you do so, it's as well to collect all the rubbish into one big pile. I know that means handling it twice, but it could take some time to unearth some of the buried 'treasure' and you won't want to do that with a skip sitting in the driveway clocking up money. Get the thing in, filled and out again as fast as you can!

Before you get rid of anything, make quite sure you can't put it to good use. If, for example, you have a slope away from the house, you may need to build up the base under the patio. To do that with concrete is expensive and all that old hardcore will do just as well.

The budget

There can't be many folk who move into a new house and find they've got money to spare! With conflicting pressures on the budget from carpets, curtains, the telephone, a new cooker and all that, the garden often has to come low down on the list of priorities. So, some careful planning is generally necessary.

Bear in mind that, even though you may have planned the finished garden, it doesn't all have to be done at once.

If you're really strapped for cash, you may, for example, decide just to cover the whole lot with grass for a year and leave it at that. Or there's an even better idea. Spend the grass-seed money on a few pounds of seed potatoes. They'll at least cover the area with green and, at the same time, they'll be effectively cleaning your land of weeds and helping to break up heavy soil. Then, when you harvest them, tot up the money you've saved and you'll find you can afford the grass seed and the paving slabs for the patio as well!

That patio is, of course, one of the most expensive items in the new garden. And there's no doubt that most of us, especially younger 'first-timers', will want a dry, hard place to eat outside, entertain friends to an alfresco barbecue or just to lie in the sun. But you can still avoid spending a fortune.

If you've bought a new house, you'll *have* to set the paving on a concrete base. I'll explain all about the reasons why later on (see page 61). So all you have to do is to make a slightly better job of the base and use that in the first year. Provided you get the levels right, you can easily cover it with paving slabs later on.

Planting is something to do slowly anyway. Often I've seen gardens of people with larger budgets and more enthusiasm than is good for them. They've had the garden 'laid out' and then gone down to the garden centre in April, on the first really sunny weekend of the year, and they've been seduced into buying everything that's in flower. They then spend the next 10 years wondering why their garden only looks good in April!

The point is that you do really need to know a little about plants before you commit yourself to filling every available space. Nonetheless, I accept that you don't want to spend months looking out at bare earth, so some colour and interest must be provided. This is what I'd do.

In the first year, buy a few packets of hardy annual seeds. Make sure the packet labels them '*hardy* annuals' because half-hardies won't come up. They can be sown directly in the soil outside and, because they're so easy to grow, success is almost guaranteed (see page 137). They'll provide a show of colour from about May through to November, giving you the whole summer to get to know a few plants and, perhaps, to save the odd bob to buy them.

In the meantime, make regular trips to garden centres, nurseries and gardens open to the public. All will give you a fascinating day out and you'll soon start noticing plants you wouldn't want to be without. Take a notebook with you and note the name and a brief description to aid your memory later on.

Of course, one thing that puts off many new gardeners is Latin names. Some of them, I agree, are a bit tortuous, but there's certainly no need to be worried about them. I do assure you that once you start to learn a few they come fairly easily. And there's a tremendous sense of superiority to be enjoyed when you can spout a few Latin names in the right company!

Another great way to fill your garden with cheap plants is to get to know other keen gardeners. If you have a gardening club in the area, it's well worth joining it. Gardeners are amongst the kindest and most enthusiastic folk in the world

It's often best in the first year to fill the borders with cheap hardy annuals raised from seed.

29

and they'll be eager to press you to accept plants they've raised themselves from seeds and cuttings, or to dig up a bit from their gardens. Later on, once you get into it, you'll want to do the same thing – guaranteed!

Tools and equipment

You simply can't make a good job of building anything, especially a garden, without the right tools. What's more, I am firmly of the opinion that it's a real false economy to buy cheap tools. So you can, I'm afraid, expect a pretty hefty outlay on tools and equipment for the garden. But, if you do it sensibly, there's still no need to give the bank manager apoplexy!

Bear in mind that many of the tools you need for the construction work can be hired. Small-tool hire shops have proliferated over the last 10 years or so and now it's possible in most towns to hire everything from a trowel to a tower crane at a fraction of the cost of buying it. Again, even the tools you *must* buy need not all be bought at once. This is what I'd suggest.

Spade

Buy this first and spend as much on it as you possibly can. You'll use it more than any other tool and if you buy a good one it'll last you a lifetime – literally. If you can run to stainless steel, do so even if you have to stretch every limit possible. It'll serve you well for ever and it'll be a perfect pleasure to use. Make sure you buy a size that suits you. Small men or slight women will be much better off with a smaller border spade than a bigger one. Above all, buy one that has been forged from steel, rather than pressed. The pressed ones are much cheaper and could, with luck, last you about a week!

Fork

Another tool you can't really do without. Again, it's worth buying a good, forged steel fork but stainless steel is an unnecessary luxury. The same rules about size and quality apply, of course.

Rake

The final member of the trio of tools you can't really do without. You'll use it extensively in the construction of the garden and it will be in constant use every season from February to November, so it's worth getting a good one.

Avoid those that look like a strip of metal with nails driven through. A solid forged job is what you want and generally it's best to go for one with 12 teeth. Again, stainless steel is unnecessary.

Shovel

When it comes to mixing concrete, you'll need a shovel. A spade is set at the wrong angle to be comfortable and you certainly won't want to be shovelling concrete with a stainless steel spade! There will be little use for it afterwards, so it's best to hire.

Hoes

There are two types of hoe, with a few odd variations you'll see from time to time. The Dutch hoe is used for general weeding – it's the one you push while walking backwards. The swan-necked or draw hoe is used for hacking out larger weeds and for making drills for seeds. Both are useful but certainly not essential. In small gardens, most of the weeding is best done by hand-pulling anyway and drills can just as well be drawn with a stick. Wait until you can easily afford them.

Trowel

A planting trowel is certainly useful, especially for women who like to keep their nails intact or where the soil is gritty or contains fragments of glass. I plant most of my small plants with my fingers but I must confess they're not fit to be seen in delicate company! Remember that trowels do have a habit of getting lost and, being small, they're easy to clean so stainless steel is not necessary, though a favourite Christmas present for new gardeners.

If you're laying paving or building walls, you will need a bricklayer's trowel and ideally, a pointing trowel too. These are best hired unless you have other work for them.

Lawn edger

Unnecessary. It's just as easy to do the job with a spade.

Secateurs

You'll certainly need them eventually, but not in the first year.

Shears

A pair of hedging shears and another to cut the edges of the

This is all it will be necessary to buy in the first year of gardening. The rest of the tool kit can be bought slowly over several years.

lawn will be useful later on, but both can certainly wait.

Sprayer

You'll use a pressure sprayer later on but initially it's probably better to hire one. The only thing you'll need it for at the construction stage is weed-killing and after that you probably won't use it for some time.

Knife

Absolutely indispensable. Buy a strong garden knife, small enough to go into your pocket without dragging your trousers off. At the same time buy a pocket carborundum stone to keep it sharp. A blunt knife is a useless embarrassment and far more dangerous than a sharp one.

Spirit-level

Indispensable in the construction stages, but expensive unless you use it for other do-it-yourself jobs. A 3-foot (90 cm) level is most useful and can be hired quite easily.

Straight-edge

For many of the construction jobs in the garden you'll need a 9 to 10 foot (3 m) straight-edge. It is simply a piece of wood, generally about 3 in × 1 in (7.5 cm × 2.5 cm) thick, which has been planed dead straight. You should be able to get the local timber merchant to machine-plane it. If you're intending to keep it for years, buy a length of hardwood since softwood will twist when it gets damp. You can, when the garden's finished, make saw-cuts at intervals to turn it into a useful planting board.

These tools will probably be necessary when you're building the garden but can be hired at a fraction of the cost of buying.

Club-hammer

A three-pound hammer is essential for paving and walling and, since you're likely to damage the handle a bit when paving (see page 66), it's only fair that you should buy rather than hire it. It'll come in very useful later and is not too expensive.

Brick bolster

You'll certainly need this to cut paving and walling slabs, but it can be hired, since you won't use it afterwards.

Wheelbarrow

If you have concrete and paving or large amounts of soil to shift, a wheelbarrow is essential. There are many different designs available, some of them quite expensive. But there still isn't one better than the builders' 'navvy barrow' which is also one of the cheapest. Buy it from the builders' merchant and make sure it has a pneumatic tyre for easy wheeling. And if you use it for wheeling concrete, make certain it's clean enough to eat out of afterwards.

Boards

When you're building the garden, wide boards are very useful indeed. If the soil is soft, they can be put down to facilitate walking and the wheeling of barrows without damaging the soil and with half the effort. Scaffold planks are ideal and can be cheaply hired. But hang on to all the old pieces of wood you come across and make a portable path a bit like a tank-track by cutting them into 2-foot (60 cm) lengths and joining them together with nylon string stapled at the ends. You'll find it invaluable for spanning wet soil without damage later on.

Lawnmower

This is one of the most expensive items you'll have to buy. If your garden is large and the budget runs to it, it's worthwhile buying a petrol-engined cylinder mower which will last many years. But the very cheap electric machines make a perfectly good job provided you expect them to last no more than about five to seven years. The points to remember are that a cylinder mower will make a finer job of the mowing but does not cope so well as a rotary with long grass. And mowers that don't pick up the cuttings are a real pain because the grass gets trodden into the house and the poor old gardener gets trodden down!

Starting with a weed-free garden will save hours of work later. Modern weedkillers will do an effective job.

Hose

I'll be going on at length about watering new plants later. Suffice it to say now that you'll need to put on a lot of water so buy a good-quality hose.

Weed control

If the plot is infested with perennial weeds, it'll pay hands down to get rid of them before you turn a spade of soil. If you do this job right at the start, you'll save yourself literally months of hand-weeding.

The easiest way is to spray the lot with a glyphosate weed-killer (Murphy Tumbleweed). It does a marvellous job, but it's by no means cheap, so it's important to use it economically. Funnily enough, my own experience has been that it also does a far *better* job when used in moderation.

First of all, choose a windless day. This is extremely important if your neighbours already have plants in their gardens. One whiff of this stuff drifting over the fence and onto their plants will knock them off too and that's not the best way to become 'Mr Popular Neighbour'!

Also make sure that it's not going to rain for at least six hours after spraying. Mix up the chemical strictly according to the makers' instructions (an extra slurp for luck is definitely *not* a good idea), and put it into a pressure sprayer. If your garden is any size at all, I would invest in one of these because you'll find a lot of use for it later. They can, however, be hired quite easily from a small-tool hire shop.

The makers do actually recommend putting it on with a watering can, but that's frankly not good advice. The weed-killer acts when it is absorbed through the leaves and transported through the plant's system to the roots. There it stops them storing food, so after a couple of weeks the plant dies. The point is that the small droplets put on with a sprayer will stick to the leaves by surface tension. But if the droplets are too large and too many they just run off into the soil where the chemical is inactivated. You'll get a poorer kill at much higher cost.

After spraying, you'll just have to contain your enthusiasm to start digging. It's essential to leave the weeds to absorb the weedkiller fully. In the summer, a couple of weeks is ample time, but in winter you'll have to wait three to four. The weeds will start to turn brown when the damage is done.

Some of the weeds that have a running root system, or storage organs below ground, like couch-grass, ground elder and bindweed, may need two or even three applications. This is not because the weedkiller is not completely effective, but because some of the roots may not have leaves above ground when you spray. So if you find, young growths coming through after spraying, you'll have to go over the plot again, just to make sure. It really is worth while.

Getting to know your soil

It's absolutely vital, now, to get to know your soil. You'll probably begin to feel pretty enthusiastic and dying to get some plants into the borders. But unless you have some idea of the stuff they're going to grow in, you could be wasting your money. And with some plants, that could be a small fortune.

The first job is to dig a hole. A favourite trick of some builders is to leave the site looking neat and tidy by bulldozing a layer of soil over the top. But that soil can hide a multitude of sins! A hole about 2 feet (60 cm) deep will soon reveal all.

Let me, first of all, paint the worst picture possible. You're unlikely to find all the disadvantages, so this way you may be able to count a blessing or two!

Imagine that the top layer of soil is yellow or grey and very sticky indeed. Underneath this is a solid layer of stone-hard soil mixed liberally with concrete, while below that is a layer of fine, crumbly brown earth. I regret to say that this is not as uncommon as you may think.

What has happened is this. The builders have used your plot to site the concrete mixer. Every night its residue of concrete has been emptied on the ground and this has hardened into a solid sheet. To make matters worse, excavators, dumper-trucks and wheelbarrows have trundled over the soil endlessly, compacting it into a hard, airless block.

Meantime, the footings for the house have been dug and the clay subsoil heaped in one corner. Once the building is finished, that subsoil is used to 'tidy up' the site, covering all the debris and mess of the whole operation.

What you are left with is a lifeless clay 'topsoil' overlying a solid rock-hard pan with the real topsoil underneath. Even if plants could grow in the clay, they could never root through the concrete to find comfort in the topsoil.

Now I must say that most modern developers have learnt this particular lesson and are a bit more careful. Many now use the garden as part of the sales package and nearly all are aware that buyers expect a much higher standard than of old.

Testing the soil is cheap and easy to do. It really is essential before buying plants.

Nonetheless, if you buy before the house is completed, it's well worth pointing out your interest in gardening and insisting on a better deal outside.

If you are faced with this worst of all situation, you have little alternative. The subsoil must be carted off and dumped. That hard pan *must* be broken up and the proper topsoil unearthed. I would love to be able to recommend a short-cut but I don't believe there is one.

Generally you'll find a much happier situation, though I must say that the hard pan caused by overcompaction is all too often in evidence. It must go, and the way to do that is by double-digging. But, before you start, there are two more tests to make to familiarise yourself properly with your soil.

Start by simply handling some of the topsoil. If, when it's moist, you can mould it into a ball like plasticine, you have a heavy clay. Now you'll hear a lot of depressing advice about the difficulties of heavy clay soil that is more or less designed to put you off for ever. Ignore it. I can tell you this; if you treat it with respect and are prepared to work at it, you'll grow much better plants in it than ever you would in sand.

If, on the other hand, the soil feels gritty when rubbed and will not hold together, there is a high sand content. This type of soil is easier to work than clay, but it's much hungrier and could well cost you more in fertiliser and manure.

If it feels silky when rubbed, the soil is silt, which should be treated very much like clay, or, unusually, you may find

There is a very wide range of superb lime-loving plants that will be much more successful on chalky soil. The lilacs are a fine substitute for rhododendrons.

a very high organic content indicating a peaty soil.

Finally, if the soil appears dry and crumbly and greyish in appearance, you are gardening on chalk. In this case you'll often be able to see pieces of white, free chalk in the soil. It's poor, dry and hungry stuff and severely restricting on the types of plants you can grow but, treated in the right way, it will still provide you with a fine garden.

Of course, these are the extremes and what you will usually find is a mixture. These soils we call 'loams'. If there is a higher proportion of clay, it's a 'heavy loam', while more sand makes it a 'light loam', and, if you're really lucky, you get the happy 'medium loam'.

The final test is for the chemical content of the soil. Very keen gardeners will want to know exactly how much of the main plant nutrients already exist in their land, and to find out you can send a sample away for analysis. Frankly, for the first-timer, that's going over the top slightly, though there is one exception. It really is absolutely vital to discover whether you garden on an acid or a chalky soil.

All plants are sensitive to the amount of lime in the soil and some so much so that they will simply die if the balance is wrong. Since a lime-test kit costs very little and is simplicity itself to use, it really is folly to buy any plants at all without knowing which will like your soil.

The simplest kits consist of a test tube into which you place a sample of your soil which has previously been air-dried. You then add a measured amount of distilled water plus a chemical provided in the kit. After a while, the soil settles to the bottom of the tube and a coloured liquid is left on top. This colour is compared with a chart to tell you the state of the soil.

The acidity is measured in terms of 'pH'. The scientific explanation of the symbol is complicated and unnecessary to understand. I never have! Suffice it to know that a pH of 7 is neutral, any figure below this being acid and any above alkaline.

Of course, to make use of these figures you need to know which plants like acid soils and which alkaline. Well, most test kits do include a list of plants and their preferences, but to make it really simple use this rule of thumb.

Most vegetables like a chalky soil so, if the pH is below 6.5, add lime to the land in the spring. The exception here is potatoes, which like an acid soil, so leave out the tatie land.

Most ornamentals either prefer or will tolerate a neutral-to-acid soil, so only add lime if the pH is very low – say below 5.0.

You will have realised that I have only talked about *raising* the pH and not about *lowering* it. This is because, while it is very easy to make soil more chalky simply by adding lime, the reverse is very difficult indeed. You can add acid peat until you're blue in the face (and red in the bank balance!) but the soil will always revert back to being chalky. While there are ways of growing acid-loving plants in chalky soil (see pages 110–113), the best bet, certainly at the outset, is to grow those plants that will do well in your soil. Instead of failing with rhododendrons, grow the beautiful lilacs instead; rather than fail with pieris, succeed with photinia. There are *always* plants that will like your soil, whatever it is.

Soil improvement

Unless you're very lucky indeed, your soil will need to be improved and 'livened up' a bit if you're to be successful with plants.

The key to improving most soils is organic matter – anything that will rot down really. Nature, of course, provides organic matter in the form of falling leaves, dying plants and animals and animal dung. Everything is recycled time and again. We need to do much the same thing but, because we expect much more from our plot of land than nature ever intended, we must use much more.

All organic matter has the effect of improving water-holding on dry soils and assisting drainage on heavy ones. It 'opens up' the soil, assisting the free passage of air and allowing young roots to work their way through the air spaces. Much organic matter contains plant foods and it also provides a home and a source of energy for millions of soil organisms that are absolutely vital to plant growth. There are several sources of organic matter.

Manure

Animal manure is by far the best soil conditioner and generally the cheapest too. It also contains quite a lot of plant food, so you'll save on fertiliser if you use it regularly. If you live in a country area where cattle are common, you'll have no problems getting hold of a trailer-load of muck quite cheaply. In the city, it's more difficult. But, even in urban areas, there's usually a riding stable or at least the odd pony or two where you can buy horse manure by the bag.

Whichever animal it comes from, all manure must be rotted for at least six months and preferably a year before use. Horse manure, particularly, is very hot when fresh and will scorch plant roots severely.

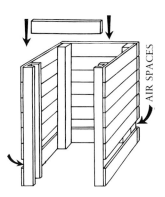

AIR SPACES

Spent mushroom compost

This is quite readily available and is a darned good soil conditioner, with one proviso. It consists of well-rotted horse manure mixed with peat but it also includes a small amount of lime. That's fine for the vegetable plot and perfectly good in borders where you're growing lime-loving plants. But, if you're blessed with a neutral or acid soil and wish to grow acid-lovers, then avoid mushroom compost. It contains very little in the way of plant food, so you'll have to add that in the form of fertiliser.

It's not difficult to knock up a compost container from old floorboards, available cheaply from a demolition contractor.

Peat

A marvellous soil conditioner which will hold several times its own weight of water, at the same time improving drainage and opening up the soil. It contains no plant food, so you'll have to add that and it has the one big drawback of cost. In my book it's a last resort because of that, but if you can afford to use it spread over the top of the borders, it sets off the plants a treat and will, of course, eventually work down into the soil.

Other alternatives

It would be true to say that anything that will rot down will improve the soil, so there are many local alternatives that can be used. Seaweed is a wonderful soil conditioner and also contains a lot of plant food. Brewers will sometimes let you have spent hops which not only do the soil a power of good but also smell great! Woollen mills throw out any amount of waste which will all rot down to improve the soil. But make quite sure it *is* wool or cotton and not a man-made fibre.

In a new garden, you naturally won't have had the opportunity of making your own organic matter in the compost heap, but you'll start collecting compostable material straightaway, so it's a good idea to invest in a container. You can buy plastic or wooden ones at the garden centre or you can make your own. All you need really is a wooden box about $2\frac{1}{2}$ feet (75 cm) square by 3 feet (90 cm) tall with a detachable front.

Special treatments

Different soils require slightly different methods of cultivation so it's as well to make a note of the basic rules.

But first of all, there's one rule that applies whether your soil is a light sand or heavy clay. Never try to cultivate it when it's soaking wet. You should even avoid walking on it if you can because, if you do, you'll force the particles together, driving out the air and making it a very inhospitable medium for plant roots.

It's not quite so bad on light soils, of course, but on heavy land, slopping about in mud will cause it to turn to concrete when it gets dry. So if you can't avoid walking on it, use boards to spread your weight.

Mind you, it can be pretty frustrating for the gardener pacing the living room, glowering out of the window at soaking wet soil and itching to get at it. There is a solution that's very practical in a small garden and will enable you to get on when you want to.

It pays hands down to invest in a big sheet of clear polythene to cover the next bit of soil you want to work on. Not only will it keep it dry but, early in the season, it'll warm it up too, so you'll be able to get planting or sowing that much sooner.

Note that I have suggested clear polythene. The black sheeting is excellent if you want to suppress weeds, especially if you can keep it there for a long time. In the end, excluding the light will conquer even the most persistent weeds. It will also keep the weather off the soil, of course, but it does nothing to warm it up.

Sand

An easy soil to work but very dry and hungry. Generally it's best to dig it over in spring when it will be easy to work up a fine, crumbly surface for sowing. It will, however, require a lot of organic matter which is probably best just put on the soil surface. It'll soon work its way in.

Clay

One of the most difficult, but eventually most rewarding, soils. Start by putting about a barrow-load of coarse grit (about the size used when tar-spraying roads) over each two or three square yards and digging it in. This will permanently help drainage. Then add as much organic matter each year as you can.

Never tread on clay soil when it's wet. Try to do all the

digging in autumn, just throwing the soil up fairly roughly. The frost and rain will break it down by spring. If you do have to tread on it, use wide boards to avoid compaction.

During the spring and summer, you'll have to choose your time for digging. You need to catch the soil in between being too wet and claggy and hard as concrete. It's an acquired art!

Try to raise borders slightly above the level of the lawn to improve drainage and grow vegetables in raised beds (see pages 180–183).

Chalk

A poor, hungry soil. It's generally dry enough to work at any time, so treat it rather like sand. You'll need all the organic matter you can lay your hands on, plus a bit more fertiliser too.

Fertilisers

All plants need feeding regularly, but you don't need a degree in chemistry to do it. Until you get specialised, two bags, or at most three, are all you'll need.

If you're intending to plant trees, shrubs, fruit trees or herbaceous plants any time between October and March, use a handful of bonemeal around each plant. This will just supply phosphate which is all that's needed at that time of year to get the roots going.

All the rest of your plants will be happy with Growmore, which is a cheap general fertiliser that contains all the major plant food necessary. Use it when planting ornamental plants and fruit in the growing season between March and October, again at about a handful per plant or, for small bedding plants, about two handfuls per square yard (sq. m). For vegetables, rake in a couple of handfuls per square yard before sowing or planting.

You'll get by perfectly happily with that formula but, if you want to be just a little more sophisticated, I would suggest that you use a rose fertiliser for all trees, shrubs and roses and also for fruit trees and bushes. It's just designed that little bit more for the job.

Double-digging

In the ornamental part of the garden, double-digging need only be done once in the life of the garden. In the vegetable plot, it's rare that it should be necessary more than once every six or seven years. All of which is just as well, because there's

1. A large plot is best divided into two.

2. Mark out each trench exactly 2 feet (60 cm) wide to ensure level digging.

3. Remove the soil one spade deep from the first trench and cart it to the final trench.

4. Break up the subsoil to the depth of the fork.

5. Put bulky organic matter in the bottom and refill the trench halfway, throwing the soil forward from the next trench.

6. Add another layer of manure and completely fill the trench. Continue working down the plot in the same way.

no hiding the fact that it's hard work!

If you have been bequeathed that hard pan below the surface, I'm afraid there's no alternative. Even under the lawn area it will cause problems with drainage that will make your grass a quagmire in wet weather.

It's a good excuse to treat yourself to a really good spade – stainless steel if you can run to it – and also make a scraper out of a bit of scrap wood. That fits into your back pocket and should be used regularly. You'll also need two canes or bits of stick 2 feet (60 cm) long and a garden line. Bear in mind, too, that when you get down to it you should go slowly and, when you feel you've had enough, take a rest, or you'll find yourself on your back for a week, cursing your luck.

Divide the whole plot into two equal halves with the garden line. The idea is to dig across half the plot at a time.

Measure the first trench using the 2-foot (60 cm) cane and

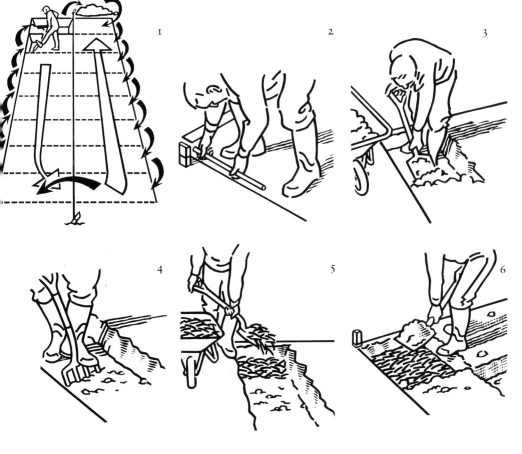

42

dig out the topsoil to the depth of the spade. This first lot must be carted or thrown onto the very end of the second half of the plot. That way it will be waiting for you ready to refill the last trench when you get to it.

After digging out the first trench, get into it and just fork over the bottom. There's no need to turn the soil over – just put the fork in to its full depth and lift the soil to break it up.

Most books will now tell you to put a layer of manure, compost or peat into the bottom of the trench. Well, that's fine if you have unlimited supplies, but few of us have. I would refill the trench at least half full and then put a bit of organic matter in where the plants will be able to reach it. I also like to put a layer on the top when the trench is refilled.

The refilling is done with the soil from the second trench which is just thrown forward. But before digging it, mark out its 2-foot (60 cm) width with the other cane. This really is quite important because it means that you refill the first trench with exactly the same amount of soil you dug out of it, so keeping the digging level.

Then simply continue in this way down the plot until you get to the end, then turn round and work back down the other half.

Single-digging is sufficient for most situations. Here the soil is dug only one spade deep and any manure put in the bottom of the trench.

Single-digging

In nine cases out of ten, this is all that's necessary. Here, you leave the subsoil alone and just turn over the topsoil. Mind you, it's still unwise to get carried away and rush at it because you're almost bound to be using muscles you never knew you had!

The easiest way is to dig out a trench right across the plot, one spade wide and one deep, throwing it evenly behind you. Then you simply work the soil forwards each time to refill the trench in front. When you get to the end, you'll be able to find enough soil from that which you threw back to refill the last trench.

It's still a good idea to use manure, peat or some other form of organic matter. Just put it in the bottom of each trench before you refill.

FENCES AND HEDGES

Ideally, the 'hard' landscaping should be done first. Jobs like paving, walling and fencing can cause havoc to existing features because it's hard to avoid wheeling barrows over the soil and slopping a bit of cement. Much better to get all that kind of work over and done with before the cultivations begin. Generally the first job is to define your boundary.

Fence or hedge?

If you have plenty of room and a little patience, a hedge is certainly the best bet. A 'living fence' looks soft and makes an ideal background for the plants in the borders. In exposed areas, hedges make the very best windbreaks too. But even a formal, clipped hedge will take up about 4 feet (120 cm) of growing room all round the garden and this is generally too much in a small plot.

Fences, on the other hand, take up little space and do have the great advantage of providing instant privacy. They may look a bit stark at first, but they can soon be softened by the use of climbing plants trained on wires fixed to the posts.

Mind you, a fence can cause problems too, and it's well worth making a good job of putting it up in the first place to avoid trouble later on. While it is certainly possible to remove and replace a rotten post, it's quite a big job and the cause of many a lost temper!

Posts generally rot at ground level, where conditions are ideal for the fungi that live on the wood. This is generally a big problem when posts are concreted into the ground. Not only does the post often rot quicker, but you're left with that massive chunk of concrete to remove before you can get the new one back in its place. It really is a headache.

But don't despair. Relatively recent developments in do-it-yourself fencing have done away with most of the problems. If you spend just a little more and follow the rules, your fence will last for many decades.

Panel fencing

There's no doubt that panel fencing is much the best bet for the do-it-yourselfer. It's not difficult to put up if you have a bit of help, there are many different styles to choose from, and modern panels are much stronger and will last a lot longer than was once the case.

When you choose panels, sort out the strongest you can find. There are still a few thin, interwoven types available and they're definitely a false economy. You may have to spend a little more on good-quality panels but they'll last much longer.

It's rare that you'll find them treated with preservative under pressure, which is the very best thing. That way they last for ever, but make sure they have at least been dipped in preservative. Painting it on afterwards is not nearly so effective. It is possible to buy posts that have been treated under pressure and they are well worth the little extra money.

One word of warning. Make sure, before you buy, that the panels have not been treated with creosote. Even the fumes will kill any plants you want to grow up the fence and may even damage those in the border close to it. Most manufacturers treat their panels with a copper or water-based preservative now, but it's worth checking, just in case.

Fences which may look hard initially can soon be softened with plants.

Fixing the posts

There are four methods of anchoring the posts into the soil and you must decide which to use before putting in your order. First of all, they can simply be put into a hole and held firm with hardcore and gravel rammed in around them. This method has the advantage that water can percolate down through the filling and will not rest around the post at soil level where it causes rotting. It requires quite a knack to get the posts firm and exactly in place, but it's a good method if you can do it.

Alternatively, you can concrete posts in. Using wet concrete which needs only gentle tamping, it's easier to get the posts exactly positioned, and this method will certainly hold even the longest fence posts firm. But it does have the snag that posts tend to rot at soil level. To reduce the risk to a minimum, put a little waterproofing agent into the mix, bring the top of the finished concrete slightly above soil level and slope it away from the post so that it will shed water.

Bear in mind that with both these methods, you'll need to order posts at least 2 feet (60 cm) longer than the panels.

The modern method of fixing is to use special sockets welded to long spikes which can be driven into the ground with a sledge-hammer. They have two great advantages. First, there are no holes to dig, so the fence can be put up much faster. Secondly, and even more important, the socket also

The easiest way to erect fencing is to drive special post sockets into the ground, but it's difficult to get the posts dead straight this way.

holds the post clear of the ground so it's unlikely to rot.

However, as you would imagine, there are disadvantages too. First, it's quite difficult to drive the spikes in accurately. Some manufacturers have made the sockets adjustable, so there there is a certain amount of leeway, but even so, it's very difficult to get a perfect result. Secondly, I'm also not at all happy about their stability. With a fence below 5 feet (150 cm) high, in solid, level soil, they're fine. But higher fences, especially in made-up or unlevel soil, tend to wave about in the breeze.

The real McCoy, as far as I'm concerned, is a combination of the two best methods – a socket that concretes into the ground. These are available and will give you the best of all worlds.

If you decide to use any of these special fixings, the posts need to be only 6 inches (15 cm) longer than the panels.

While you're ordering, you'll also need a supply of special brackets to fix the panels to the posts. They are a *great* advance on the old method of nailing through the side rail of the panel (which always has a habit of splitting), and well worth a little extra outlay. You'll want fixing screws too, and, if you're using concrete, some ballast and cement.

Building the fence

The first thing is to measure your boundary accurately, and that's a lot more important than you may appreciate. Nothing gets folk more worked up than the thought that their neighbour may be pinching a little bit of their land. I have known full-scale feuds between neighbours over no more than an inch of soil.

And once you've decided on the dividing line, remember that your fence must go *your* side of that line. It's also customary to give your neighbour the 'smooth' side of the fence. All panel fences have one side with struts and one side without and, though I know of no legal requirement, it seems that it's the normal practice to put the struts on your side. But, whatever you do, when you come to fix the panels, make sure you get them all the same way round. I know it sounds impossible, but I once finished a fence only to find that I'd put just one panel in the wrong way round! And it's a devil of a job to get it out again.

Mark out the line with a garden line made with strong nylon twine and then set the first post. If you are driving in spikes, simply bang the spike down so that the base-plate rests on the ground, slot in the post and, if it's adjustable, tighten up the nuts.

If you're ramming in hardcore, you'll need to dig a hole about 18 inches (45 cm) deep and as narrow as you can make it. Put the post in, put a little hardcore round it and ram it down. Gradually fill to the top, ramming as you go. It's important with this method to check regularly with a spirit-level that the post is upright both ways.

Concreting the posts in is easier. Use a mix of 6 parts by volume ballast to 1 part Portland cement with a little waterproofing liquid added to the water. Make the mix as dry as you can, consistent with it being workable. Again, dig a hole 18 inches (45 cm) deep and as narrow as you can and put a little concrete in the bottom of the hole before setting the post. This is important because it means that the post will be totally encased in waterproof concrete which will stop water rising up through it and rotting it. Put the post in the centre and fill round with concrete, ramming and checking for straightness as you go.

When the concrete is at the required height, make sure you slope the top of it so that water will run away from the post, to avoid rotting.

If you're using one of the sockets that can be concreted in, the hole can be a bit shallower – say about 1 foot (30 cm) deep – provided that the soil is firm. The best way is to fix the socket to the post before you put it into the ground. That way you can make sure, with the spirit-level, that the socket is in the right position to ensure that the post is upright.

The golden rule with fencing is to put posts and panels up together as you go. It really is virtually impossible to put all the posts in first and then hope to fit the panels afterwards. You only need to be a fraction of an inch out, and you'll have to start cutting panels or nailing strips on. Much better to be on the safe side.

So if you are working with the special spikes, the next job is to fix the panel to the post. You can nail it on, but the special fixing brackets now supplied by some manufacturers are much better.

Make sure that the panel is at least 3 inches (7.5 cm) off the ground to avoid rotting. I do this with a couple of bricks underneath the panel, and these have to be packed with bits of wood to get each panel exactly right.

If you're concreting posts in, or ramming in hardcore, you'll find it easier to dig the second hole before the panel is fixed.

1. Fix the special sockets to the posts.
2. Check that the post is upright, fill round the socket with concrete and tamp down hard.
3. Fix the panels to the posts. They can be nailed, but brackets are better.
4. Ensure that the post is upright; hold it in place with a spare post.

The best way is to measure the distance either with the capping strip supplied for the panels or, if they're nailed on and not supplied separately, with the panel itself. Then fix the panel as before, supporting the loose end on a brick packed with pieces of wood to bring it dead level.

Now the second post is fixed to the other end of the panel in exactly the same way as the first. Be careful to ensure that the second post is at exactly the right height. If the panel is levelled before fixing, you can do this by measuring from the top of the panel to the top of the post. I carry a 2-inch (5 cm) piece of wood in my pocket for the purpose.

If the posts are concreted in, you'll need to support each panel until the concrete is hard. This can be done with the fencing posts you haven't yet used. Just bang a nail in so that it projects at the end and lean it against the panel so that the nail hooks over it. Check again that the posts are level and leave it like this for at least 24 hours. When you get to the end of the job, you'll naturally have to find a few spare bits of wood to use as props.

At the end of the run, you'll find that the last panel won't fit. If it does, someone, somewhere, is certainly watching over you! Ordinary mortals will have to do some cutting.

Start by carefully measuring the space you need to fill. Then lever off the slats on one end of the panel. A big screwdriver and a claw-hammer will generally do the trick quite easily.

Mark the extent of the new size and nail the two struts back on again in the new position. You'll find you need to do this on a hard surface; a scaffold plank resting on the soil will do well. If the panel is more than half its original size, you'll need to shift the centre struts in the same way too, just to make it look uniform.

With the struts nailed on to their new position, the excess bit of panel can be cut off and discarded and the new-sized piece fixed in the space.

All that remains is to nail the caps onto the posts with a couple of 2-inch (5 cm) nails apiece and, if they come separately, the capping strips on the panels, and the job's done.

Most 'coffee-table' garden designers treat panel fencing with a grand contempt, but I must say that I agree with them on one point only. The colour – usually a vivid orange – is pretty revolting and not at all an attractive background for plants. However, there are several stains that are harmless to plants and will give the effect of instant weathering. Your builders' merchant or do-it-yourself store will stock a range of different colours which, for my money, make all the difference.

Stepped fencing

If your garden slopes, you'll have to make special provisions. Obviously you can't allow the panels to follow the line of the slope, or the posts will go in at an angle! So the panels have to be 'stepped' at intervals.

It's a good idea to work out the extent of the slope before ordering the panels. This is because each 'step' will require a longer post, so you need to know how many there'll be. You can do this with a straight-edge, a spirit-level and a number of pegs. Start at the highest end and put the straight-edge on the ground. The other end should rest on a peg which is hammered in until it's level. On a long garden you may need several pegs, with the height of the last one from the ground indicating the extent of the slope.

Ideally, each step should not exceed about 6 inches (15 cm) or the space under the panel will be too great. Starting at the lowest point, set the first panels in the normal way until you find you have to dig out soil to keep the panel level. Then it's time to step up 6 inches (15 cm). When you reach this stage, don't forget that you'll need a post 6 inches (15 cm) longer than you've been using.

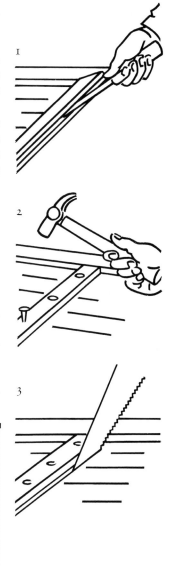

1. Remove the end struts from a complete panel, levering them up with a screwdriver.
2. Measure the required length and re-nail the struts in position both sides.
3. Saw off the excess and the panel will fit exactly.
4. On sloping ground, fencing must be stepped. Fill in the holes at the bottom with gravel-boards.

Gravel boards

Naturally, if you step up, you'll have a gap underneath the fence of 6 inches (15 cm) at one end of the panel, tapering down to nothing at the other. This space can be filled with a gravel board. Indeed, I like to use gravel boards in any case. Remember that it's invariably the bottom of the panel that rots first, because it's here that rain and soil splash up or soil get piled against the panel. If rotting occurs on the panel, you have a major and an expensive job on your hands. But the gravel board is only 6 inches (15 cm) wide and easy and cheap to replace.

If you have concreted the posts into the ground, or used the rammed hardcore method, all you need do is to dig out sufficiently to enable the 6 in × 1 in × 6 ft (15 cm × 2.5 cm × 180 cm) board to slide under the panel. It is fixed by nailing a 1 in × $1\frac{1}{2}$ in (2.5 cm × 4 cm) block onto the post and then nailing the gravel board to the block.

If you have used metal sockets, the job is complicated by the fact that the socket prevents you nailing into the post. In this case fix the gravel board with a couple of metal brackets from the panel to the top of the board. You can buy brackets at most ironmongers or builders' merchants.

Other types of fencing

The cheapest fence I ever put up was one of the most attractive and durable. I made it with second-hand timber bought from the demolition contractor's yard for a fraction of the cost of proper fencing.

You need for the posts 3 in × 3 in (7.5 cm × 7.5 cm) floor joists; for the rails, 3 in × 2 in (7.5 cm × 5 cm) joists; plus floorboarding at whatever size you can get hold of.

The posts are put in as previously described, about 8 to 9 feet (250 cm) apart, and the rails are simply bolted on with 6-inch (15 cm) coach bolts. If you're a competent carpenter, you may prefer to make proper half joints, but it's not really necessary. The only thing to watch is that, if your posts have been set right up to the edge of your boundary, you must bolt the rails on your side of the fence or you'll be trespassing on your neighbour's land.

Then simply cut the floorboards to the required lengths and nail them on. It's best to put a small gap of about 1 inch (2.5 cm) between each board. This looks better and also filters the wind through.

Naturally, the fence will need treating with a preservative afterwards, so make sure again that it's water or copper based.

Paling fences are put up in much the same way. You can buy palings at most timber merchants or do-it-yourself stores and they look quite attractive, though naturally they have their limitations. Over about 4 feet (120 cm) high they begin to look wrong and they also offer no privacy.

Wattle fencing makes a very attractive boundary and a good windbreak in country gardens. Makers and suppliers are few and far between, but some still advertise in gardening magazines.

Nothing could be simpler to put up. Just drive round posts into the ground at the required distances and wire the panels to them. The great limitation of wattle fencing is that it will rarely last more than about 10 years.

The lower fence at the side is made from hazel wattles, while the taller one is home-made using old floorboards from the demolition contractor.

Trellis

Square or diamond-shaped trellis makes an attractive fence within the garden, its openness creating a much softer effect. It can be used to support plants, of course, yet still allows a glimpse through, here and there, adding to the illusion of extra space.

Trellis can also be used to good effect to top panel fencing, adding height without increasing the 'boxed-in' effect. This is the way we shut out the dreaded chemical factory which provided the 'view' from our Birmingham garden. The panel manufacturers generally make square trellis panels to fit their fencing and in various heights, normally increasing in 1-foot (30 cm) increments. Naturally the posts must be long enough to take the extra trellis which is simply placed on top and nailed through the side-struts to the posts.

This square trellis has the advantage of being thicker than normal diamond trellis which is not really suitable for use as fencing. That is intended to be fixed to battens on a wall where it will receive less buffeting from winds and can be fixed at closer intervals.

It's also possible to buy tailor-made panels to fit any particular location. These panels are made in traditional styles and are very beautiful indeed. Unfortunately, so is the price! However, with care, a competent do-it-yourselfer could make his or her own.

Making rectangular panels is straightforward, provided you remember to drill the thin lathes before nailing or screwing through them. Curves require patience. You'll find that if you make a series of saw-cuts about three quarters of the way through the lathe and about an inch (2.5 cm) apart, you'll be able to bend them sufficiently. Naturally the bend should be such that the cuts are on the inside of the curve and so close

Trellis makes a useful extension to the fence without increasing the 'closed-in' effect. Note the attractive curve where the fence changes height.

A wrought-iron gate will not provide privacy but gives an attractive glimpse of the garden beyond.

up rather than open. You can buy ready-made mouldings and wooden balls to embellish the trellis from the better timber merchants.

Gates

In a large garden a gate can be a delightful feature. There's something of a sense of mystery about a closed gate and the view immediately after opening it should reflect that. What's more, a half-open, or a wrought-iron gate with the glimpse of a beautiful border beyond tempts you to walk on to discover further delights. Alas, all this is somewhat fanciful in a small garden.

Generally, modern gardens can be seen in their entirety at a glance and there is little scope for mystery or surprise. In this case, make the gate relatively unobtrusive by using the same materials as the fence.

Gates in walls can be made of wrought iron, which allows a glimpse of the garden beyond. If you do use one, plan for some bulky planting beyond, which will add to the illusion of space and also provide privacy.

Hanging a gate is a simple and straightforward operation. Fix the hinges to the gate first, then put a piece of wood at least 1 inch (2.5 cm) thick on the ground between the gateposts to allow adequate clearance beneath the gate when it's fixed. Offer it up to the gatepost and screw the hinges to the post.

It is very important, though, to make sure that the gatepost itself is strong and well anchored. There are few things more annoying than having to struggle to lift a gate off the ground before it can be opened. Try doing it with an armful of parcels!

Wrought-iron gates are often fixed directly to a wall. In this case it's necessary to hack out a hole with a masonry drill and cold chisel. Make it plenty big enough to take both the hinge fixing and a generous amount of cement and use sharp sand mixed 3:1 with cement for a really strong job. Allow at least three days for the cement to harden before hanging the gate.

If you have young children, you should also make sure that the latch is fitted at a height they can't reach. It saves an awful lot of worry, especially if you live near a busy road.

Sometimes there is a temptation to emulate the 'stately homes' by making an imposing entrance to the garden of a small house. You've seen them too, with impressive stone pillars topped by pineapples or recumbent lions. While I strongly believe that gardens are personal things and no one should set themselves up as arbiters of good or bad 'taste', let me just urge you to think carefully before doing anything quite as grand. A sense of proportion is a wonderful thing!

Hedging

There's nothing quite like a good hedge to set off a garden, but there are two things you *must* have – space and patience. Whatever the advertisements in the Sunday papers may say, it will take at least three and probably five years for any hedge to reach 6 feet (180 cm) and it will take up a considerable area all round the garden. But if you can do it, then I urge you to have a go.

There are two broad categories of hedging – formal and informal. Basically a formal hedge is one that will stand clipping and can therefore be kept more compact. An informal hedge is simply a line of shrubs allowed to grow more or less naturally with just a little pruning from time to time. They take up much more room, depending on the one you choose, but they do have the great advantage that they will flower in season.

Before you choose a hedging plant, ask yourself what you're expecting of it. You're likely, for example, to want it to shield your garden from the view of passers-by or from the neighbours. A little privacy in the garden, after all, is a pretty necessary thing, In that case, you'll need something that will grow as fast as possible and to at least 6 feet (180 cm). Ideally it should also be evergreen or at least thick enough to protect you from view in the winter.

You may need a hedge to protect your garden from winds. If you do, you'll have to worry in the early stages about a windbreak to protect the windbreak! But more of that later. Make sure, in any case, that the plants you choose are hardy enough to do the job.

Finally, you may be anxious to keep out wandering dogs, cats or children. Indeed, you may even want to keep them in! So your choice then might be a plant equipped with the discouragement of fierce thorns. There are hedging plants available that would keep out an elephant, let alone the ginger tom from next door.

The main criterion, of course, will be aesthetic, so it's a good idea to go along to a few mature gardens to see what the plant looks like 10 or more years after planting.

Formal hedges

Clipped hedges will be the choice of most first-time gardeners because they take up much less room. First of all, don't, for heaven's sake, be worried about all the work they entail. Ever since the appearance in garden centres of a chemical that slows down the growth of hedges, gardeners have got the impression that they take hours and hours of maintenance. In fact, most need clipping once a year and others, at the most, three times. And with shears or electric clippers, it's easy work and a great pleasure. Don't be worried about the Latin names either. The first one on my list is a real off-putter!

Leyland's Cypress (Cupressocyparis leylandii)
This is more often simply called 'Leylandii'. It's probably the most reviled conifer in recent times and, in my view, quite wrongly. One reason is that there are several different 'strains' of 'Leylandii', some of which are pretty indifferent. However, most nurserymen now stick to two types which are more compact and make excellent hedges, so the looser, floppier 'Leylandii' hedges of the past are no more.

Certainly it has been very widely planted because of its fast growth, so plant snobs should perhaps look for something less common. Nevertheless, it's a first-rate plant. After a year establishing itself, it will grow 2 to 3 feet (60–90 cm) a year to produce a good, matt background for border plants. And it can be clipped very hard indeed, provided you start early enough in the life of the plants. I've seen hedges 8 feet (240 cm) tall and only 2 feet (60 cm) wide at the base, narrowing to 6 inches (15 cm) at the top. And they looked stunning!

There is also a bright golden form called 'Castlewellan Gold' which grows very nearly as fast and certainly brightens the place up. Some folk plant the green and gold alternately to give a kind of mottled effect. I don't like it but that's no reason why you shouldn't.

Plant both kinds 3 feet (90 cm) apart.

Western Red Cedar (Thuja plicata)
In my view, one of the best of hedging conifers. There's a variety called 'Atrovirens' which, for some reason, is grown widely in France but not so much here. It is available, however, and makes a lovely bright, fresh green hedge. It's not quite so fast as 'Leylandii', growing about $1\frac{1}{2}$ to $2\frac{1}{2}$ feet (46–76 cm) a year, but well worth the wait.

Thujas have one other great advantage too. They will shoot again from inside the plant if the outside gets scorched from wind or cold. So if your hedge turns browns and dead on the outside in a very hard winter, you can be happy that it will come back eventually.

Plant 3 feet (90 cm) apart.

Yew (Taxus baccata)

The real aristocrat of conifer hedges. It's slower growing than the others but will make about 1 foot (30 cm) a year for the first five or six years. Nonetheless, you'll need a little patience for a fully established, thick hedge. But if ever a hedge was worth waiting for, this is it. It forms a dense, impenetrable, matt green wall which can be clipped to perfection. It's hardy, tolerant of most garden soils and will live for a thousand years!

Plant 2 feet (60 cm) apart.

Beech (Fagus sylvatica)

Often a more realistic hedge than the conifers because of the cost. Buy bare-rooted plants in autumn and you'll do it a *lot* cheaper. Though not evergreen, beech retains its dead leaves all winter until the new ones push them off in the spring. This gives a superb russet brown screen, which makes a pleasant winter difference to the fresh green of the spring and summer growth. It will put on about 1 to $1\frac{1}{2}$ feet (30–46 cm) of growth a year once established. One word of warning: this is one plant that should not be trimmed until it has reached its required height.

If it has a snag, it's that it really requires a light, well-drained soil. If yours isn't, you'd be well advised to grow the similar hornbeam instead. There is also a copper-leaved variety which is perhaps very slightly slower in growth and a bit more expensive, but looks splendid.

Plant 2 feet (60 cm) apart.

Hornbeam (Carpinus betula)

A less demanding plant than beech, but with much the same appearance though lacking just a little sparkle. The dead leaves in winter don't have quite as bright a russet colour and the new foliage is perhaps not quite so fresh-looking. Still, a much better bet on heavy soil.

Plant 2 feet (60 cm) apart.

Laurel (Prunus laurocerasus 'Rotundifolia')

This, in my view, makes a really striking hedge. The bright, glossy green leaves are quite big so they sparkle dramatically

Above. A hedge of Leyland's cypress makes an attractive, fast-growing hedge which can be closely clipped.

Right. Beech is one of the best garden hedges. It isn't evergreen but it retains its old, russet-coloured leaves all winter.

in the sun. There's something very pleasing about the sight of a well-grown, vigorous, healthy bush and laurel always seems to look that way. It will grow about 1 to $1\frac{1}{2}$ feet (30–46 cm) a year and requires trimming only once. But, when you do, it's a secateur job rather than shears I'm afraid. If you cut through the leaves with shears, the jagged scars look ugly. It has the one other disadvantage that it's expensive – but well worth saving for.

Plant 3 feet (90 cm) apart.

Hawthorn (Crataegus monogyna)
This is a common field hedge, but I include it here because it's one of the cheapest and can make a very good animal-proof hedge. However, it *must* be cut back hard after planting and about halfway each year to keep it bushy at the bottom.

Plant 1 foot (30 cm) apart.

Privet (Ligustrum ovalifolium)
I include this only to say don't grow it unless you have a very large garden. It makes a wonderful, fast-growing hedge, but it's so hungry it will rob the soil of all water and plant food for a couple of yards around it. That's just too much competition for most plants. There is also a yellow form which is, alas, just as greedy.

If you do buy a stately home, plant 1 foot (30 cm) apart.

Informal hedges
Since an informal hedge is simply a line of shrubs, you could, I suppose, use almost anything you like. However, as these

will take up a lot of space, it's a lucky gardener who can indulge in one. My list is fairly short for that reason.

Barberry (*Berberis*)

If you want to keep the Russians out of your garden, *Berberis julianae* will certainly stop a nuclear missile! The thorns are such that nothing goes near, let alone through. It's evergreen and sports marvellous yellow flowers in spring, but it's a bit painful to prune.

Barberries make attractive, animal-proof hedges which, though generally grown informally, can also be clipped.

B. *stenophylla* is often grown as hedging and produces large, graceful, arching branches covered in yellow flowers in April. The spines are not quite so painful.

B. *thunbergii* 'Atropurpurea' has red foliage and yellow flowers in spring.

Plant 3 feet (90 cm) apart.

Laurustinus (*Viburnum tinus*)

A popular winter-flowering evergreen which will form a bushy hedge up to about 6 feet (180 cm) high. The large heads of flowers start as pink buds and open to white. They appear continuously from late autumn to early spring. A really excellent hedge even in shade. The variety 'Eve Price' is one of the best.

Plant 3 feet (90 cm) apart.

Roses (*Rosa rugosa*)

Often advertised as a wonderful flowering hedge, but leaves

For a low-growing hedge, lavender, with its grey, aromatic foliage and blue summer flowers, is hard to beat.

57

a lot to be desired in my opinion. Straggly in growth and fairly sparse in flower, not evergreen and prone to pest and disease attack, it's one advertisement not to be taken in by.

Low-growing hedges

Sometimes, a hedge is used not for screening or shelter, but simply as a decorative edging to a path or border. Often herb gardens are set out in a formal way using a close-clipped, dwarf hedge to mark the separate beds. If you're really ambitious, you could make a smaller version of the Elizabethan 'knot-garden'. This attractive floral feature looks at home even in modern gardens. Naturally, the hedge must be dwarf and it must respond to heavy clipping.

Box (*Buxus sempervirens 'Suffruticosa'*)

The edging box makes a perfect dwarf hedge with its dark, shiny leaves which respond well to clipping. It roots easily from cuttings just stuck in the ground, so you can save money by buying a couple of plants and raising the rest yourself. This is the most popular plant for knot gardens and formal herb gardens.

Plant 6 inches (15 cm) apart.

Lavender (*Lavandula angustifolia*)

One of the most attractive dwarf hedges, with smoky grey foliage and masses of insect-attracting blue flowers in summer. Go for the more compact varieties like 'Hidcote' or 'Munstead' and trim the plants over after flowering to prevent them becoming straggly.

Plant 1 foot (30 cm) apart.

Cotton lavender (*Santolina chamaecyparissus*)

The dense, silvery foliage alone makes this plant worthwhile and the bright, lemon-yellow flowers are a welcome summer bonus. Again, trim back after flowering.

Plant 1 foot (30 cm) apart.

Planting hedges

Obviously, the name of the game with hedges is fast growth, so it's worth going to town over the preparation of the soil.

Mark out the line and dig a trench at least 2 feet (60 cm) wide, throwing the soil out to one side. Fork over the bottom to break up the subsoil and then put a good layer of organic matter into the bottom. Ideally, use well-rotted manure; if you can't get hold of it, you'll have to use peat. Put back half the soil and then add another layer of organic matter. Then completely refill and spread a bit more organic material on the top. You'll find, of course, that the top of the planting line is now well above the surrounding soil, so preferably leave it to settle for a few weeks.

The best time for planting is in the autumn. The soil will be warm then and the plants will make some roots before the cold weather sets in. They'll be on their marks then for a fast start in the spring. What's more, in the autumn you can buy plants either bare-rooted or root-wrapped, which is quite a bit cheaper than buying them in containers. Before planting, dust the soil with bonemeal, using about two handfuls per yard (metre) run.

Whichever plants you use, set them at the appropriate distances apart and exactly at the level they grew on the nursery. With small, bare-rooted plants, I just cut a slit with the spade, whack the roots in with a flick of the wrist, to make sure they hang downwards, remove the spade and put my boot on the roots. It really is as easy as that. Root-wrapped plants will require a larger hole.

If you do buy plants out of the dormant season they'll have to be in containers, and here there's one very important point to watch. It's a strange fact that, once the roots of a plant fill the container and then start going round the bottom of the pot, they tend to continue to do so – just as if they get dizzy and can't stop.

They will also continue the habit once they get into the soil. This means that they fail to spread out to provide proper anchorage. So it has been known for some plants, particularly conifers, to reach 6 or 8 feet (180–240 cm) and then just blow over. On inspection, the roots have been like a corkscrew, offering little or no anchorage.

So check the root systems of container-grown plants when you're planting and, if they have started to encircle the pot, gently tease them out before putting them in the ground.

Pruning

After planting hawthorn and privet, it's best to cut them back hard – to within about 2 inches (5 cm) of the ground. This may seem like defeating the fast-growth objective, but it will give you a much bushier, closer hedge, with branches and foliage right down to the base. I would also cut back each year's growth by about a third every autumn until the plants

Once the soil is prepared, the plants are easy to put in by cutting a slit with a spade.

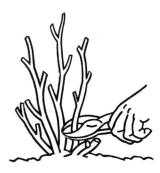

To encourage bushy growth right down at ground level, it's best to prune some hedging plants really hard.

have reached the required height. Then trim as needed to keep them tidy; start in May or June, depending on growth.

Beech and hornbeam should not have their tops cut back until they reach the required final height. However, the sides can be lightly trimmed after the second season after planting.

Conifers must have their sides trimmed back early in their lives. Start cutting back lightly in the second season, continually trimming back rampant growth. If you don't, the inside of the plant will go bare and you'll have lost your chance. Don't cut back the tops until they've reached the required height.

The one exception here is yew, which seems to thrive on cutting back. If you've got the patience, cut back about a third of the current season's growth each year. The best time to prune conifers is the early part of August.

Windbreaks

If your hedge is to be used as a windbreak, you'll have to protect it in the early years. Conifers are particularly susceptible to wind damage, which dehydrates them and turns them brown. Ideally, erect a screen made of plastic windbreak material on the windward side. Unfortunately, windbreaks need strong supports and they don't look too pretty while they're up – which should be about 18 months if you plant in the autumn. But you could lose your plants if you don't protect them.

Aftercare

In the early stages, water is absolutely essential, especially if the plants were container-grown. Check regularly and make sure they never go dry.

Hedges often get neglected when the fertiliser bag's going round. Like all plants, they need feeding and an annual dose of fertiliser will make all the difference to their speed of growth. They'll certainly repay you.

Use a rose fertiliser applied in late February at about two handfuls every yard (metre) run of hedge.

Hedges can attract wildlife but can also harbour pests and diseases. On balance, I would clean out any rubbish that collects at the bottom of the hedge each autumn – after first carefully checking for signs of hedgehogs!

Opposite. Paving slabs look very attractive when laid in an entirely random pattern.

PAVING

Before you start to lay any kind of paving, there are two things you *must* get right. Neglect either of them and your paving will be a thorn in your flesh for ever more. What's more, you must studiously ignore all the advice you'll get (oh, yes you will!) about short cuts. Paving is expensive, and it's hard work. The only way to do it is the right way – first time.

The first golden rule is to get your levels right. Take meticulous care about this job because 'as near as dammit' simply won't do. At best you'll have a patio that's swimming in water. At worst you'll find damp creeping inside the house and rotting the carpets.

Secondly, make quite sure that the base is solid. This is especially important in new gardens, where the footings of the house have been dug out with an oversized mechanical shovel. After the walls are built, the shovel then pushes the soil back into the trench where it will continue to settle for a considerable time.

You may have seen the local council pavers laying slabs on sand when they repair the pavement. But remember that they're doing it on soil that has been compacted for many years. Unless yours has too, you *must* use something more substantial. Otherwise the slabs will sink unevenly, and they'll tip up all over the place, creating highly dangerous 'trips', and you'll find yourself starting again.

Rectangular paving

Rectangular slabs certainly constitute the most popular form of paving and with good reason. For the do-it-yourselfer, they're about the easiest to lay, there's a vast range to choose from and they suit modern architecture and materials extremely well. You won't think they're cheap until you begin to compare them with other materials, when they begin to look very attractive indeed!

The easiest way to lay them is in straight lines and, if you choose square slabs, nothing could be easier. This looks fine on a small area and is the pattern we chose for our small quadrant of paving outside the patio doors. On a larger area, you may choose to use slabs of varying sizes laid in a 'random' pattern to eliminate the 'tram-line' effect. It's a softer finish which will harmonise well with plants.

If you decide to do it this way, you must either work out a pattern of paving on paper first and order the appropriate amount of slabs or simply work it out as you go along. The latter way you get a *really* random effect, but you must be careful how you order. If there are three or four different sizes, make sure you order equal *areas* of each size rather than equal numbers. Otherwise you'll find you finish up with far too many larger sizes.

If you're paving in a shady part of the garden, it's a good idea to use a slab with a non-slip finish. Without sun, slabs tend to get a thin covering of green algae which makes them very slippery and dangerous.

You may also need to do a bit of cutting. If you've been blessed with inspection covers where you intend to pave, you can expect to have to cut the paving round them. In this case, it could save some money to buy paving slabs that will cut easily with a hammer and brick bolster. While an angle grinder will cut through any slab, they have to be hired and you'll have to buy at least one disc however little cutting you need to do.

Getting the levels

This is the most important part of the job and even more so if the paving runs alongside the house. It's well worth taking time and trouble over it.

Start by finding the damp-proof course (D P C) on the house. This is a waterproof membrane built into the house wall to stop rising damp. On modern houses it's easily recognised as a wider course of mortar between the bricks. Some older

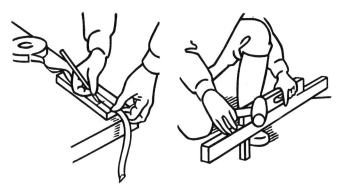

1. Cut pegs and mark them with a clear line 3 in (7.5 cm) from the top.
2. Level the first peg so that it's two courses of bricks below the damp-proof-course.

houses use a row of blue engineering bricks which are, of course, even easier to see. Whichever way it's done, the top level of the finished paving must come at least two courses of bricks, (6 to 7 inches (15–18 cm)) below the DPC. That will cope with flash floods and rain splashing up from the paving above the DPC.

Now cut yourself some decent pegs. They'll need to be about 1 to 1½ feet (30–45 cm) long with a clean square top. Mark a clear line on each peg 3 inches (8 cm) from the top which will give a guide for the level of the concrete base later.

After marking out the shape of the paved area, bang the first peg into the ground 1 foot (30 cm) away from the house wall. Using a spirit-level, make sure the top finishes exactly two courses of bricks below the DPC. Then, using a straight-edge and spirit-level, put in a line of pegs about 4 feet (120 cm) apart and also 1 foot (30 cm) from the wall and, of course, all at exactly the same level as the first.

The second row of pegs must be slightly lower than the first. It's important to ensure that water runs away from the house, so the paving must slope very slightly. Make the second row about 4 feet (120 cm) from the first and set the pegs about half an inch (13 mm) lower. You can do this by putting a half-inch (13 mm) thick piece of wood on the second peg as you level it. Get it exactly level with the first peg, remove the block and it will be half an inch (13 mm) lower. The second row can then be put in, checking the level against the first peg in the row and, with the aid of the bit of wood, with the other pegs in row one. A third and possibly a fourth row of pegs follow, depending on the width of the patio.

When the pegs are all in, make quite sure that you put the work area strictly out of bounds to the rest of the family.

1. Mix the ballast and cement dry and spread it on the site.
2. Tread it down hard making sure it comes up to the marks on the pegs.

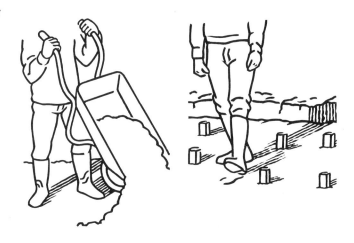

Those pegs are very easy to trip over, causing injury and up-setting your levels too! As it is, you're bound to trip over one or two yourself before you finish the job!

Making the base
Generally there will be quite a bit of digging out to do to allow a good thickness of concrete for the base. You'll need at least 3 inches (8 cm) so the soil must be dug out to that depth below the line marked on the pegs.

When you're digging, try not to go too deep so that you have to refill, but, if you do, fill up either with hardcore or concrete. If you put soil back into the hollows, you'll only increase the sinkage problem. The same rule applies, of course, if the soil is too low in the first place. It must be made up with some hard material which is not subject to settlement. If you're moving into a house on an estate development, you'll almost certainly find plenty of hardcore about.

The base should always be made with concrete unless you're certain that the site has been compacted and undis-turbed for years. You may, for example, wish to pave an existing gravel path, in which case the concrete base is unnecessary.

In fact, laying the base is not as arduous as it sounds. It's perfectly OK to mix the concrete dry, which is much less of a back-break than using wet concrete.

What I do is this. Put four shovels of ballast into a wheel-barrow and cover it with half a shovel of cement. Mix that about a bit in the barrow and then add another four shovels of ballast and a half of cement. Another little mix and top it off with two shovels of ballast.

Then wheel the lot to where you want it, tip it and rake it out. All this moving about will mix the ingredients together quite enough. Tread it down firmly by walking all over every square inch with your weight on your heels and then just level the top with the rake, so that the concrete comes to the mark on the pegs. And that's it. It won't be long before the moisture from below creeps up and that from above works down, to harden up the whole thing. The one exception to this rule is when you've opted to delay the paving and to use the concrete base as the patio initially, as suggested before (see page 29). In this case, you'll need to provide a wooden 'shuttering' to edge the patio. Set this level across the house and with a slight slope away from it. Make the concrete wet enough to work and level it with a board spanning the shuttering.

1. Start near the wall and set out five heaps of mortar for the first slab.

Laying the slabs

Now for the exciting bit. The slabs are laid on mortar, using a mixture of builders' sand and cement. Mix three parts of sand to one of cement and make it a fairly dry mix. It's not difficult to imagine what happens when the mortar is too wet. You place the slab on top of it and the whole lot instantly collapses to below the required height. It *must* be stiff enough to support the weight of the slabs.

Start with a slab at one end of the area and, if you're paving next to the house, it should be one of the rows nearest the wall. Take a lot of trouble over this first slab because it will set the pattern for all the rest.

Put down five little mounds of mortar, one for each corner of the slab and one in the middle. Make the mounds about 4 inches (10 cm) high to allow plenty of tapping down. Now rest the slab gently on top of the piles in roughly the right position. It needs to run exactly parallel to the wall and you should also exercise a little caution – pessimism if you like. At the end of the job, you'll be pleased you started off looking on the black side!

Imagine how easy it is to get that first slab just, say, an eighth of an inch (3 mm) out of line with the wall. Well, if the slab is 2 feet (60 cm) long and the whole paved area is 20 feet (6 m), you'll be 10 times that amount out of line by the time you get to the end. So take care to get it right.

To make sure, set the slab 1 inch (2.5 cm) away from the wall. Then wrap one end of a nylon bricklayer's line round a

2. Carefully lay the first slab on the heaps of mortar.

1. Take extra trouble to get the first slab square with the house and level with the pegs.

2. Now the remainder of the slabs are laid in the same way, butting them up against each other.

brick and fix it so that it runs along the back line of the slab. Hold it in place with another brick resting on the slab. Take the line to the other end of the paving and hold it exactly 1 inch (2.5 cm) away from the wall. It should then run exactly along the back edge of the slab. If it doesn't, tap the slab into line and check again.

Now check for level by putting a straight-edge onto the top of the slab and the nearest peg. Tap the slab down until the straight-edge lies flush along the surface of the slab. Repeat the process with other pegs you can reach to make quite certain the slab is level all ways. Then recheck the line against the wall and you can feel satisfied you've got it right. After that first one it's all plain sailing.

The tapping down is best done with the handle of a 3 lb (1.3 kg) club-hammer (or 'lump' hammer in some parts of the country). Never use the metal head or you'll damage the surface of the slabs and could crack them. Constant use will certainly ruin the handle but it will be neither difficult nor expensive to replace.

3. The easiest way to cut slabs is with an angle grinder which you can hire.

With the first slab in place, there's no need now to check for line again, because you simply butt the next slab up against it and continue in that way. However, it is always necessary to check for level. Do it from pegs in both directions for each slab you lay.

If you're laying slabs in a purely random pattern which has not been worked out in advance, you'll have to think a couple of slabs ahead each time. Try to avoid long 'tram-lines'. As soon as you see a line between two rows of slabs becoming too long, make sure you break it by putting a slab across it. This does take a bit of thought, but it's great fun to work out!

Cutting slabs

Unless you're very lucky (or perhaps very clever!) you'll almost certainly have to cut a slab or two. It may be right at the end to make it fit in, or you may have to cut around an inspection cover or a downpipe.

Most precast slabs are not difficult to cut in straight lines with a brick bolster and club-hammer. But if you have any fancy cutting to do, you'll be well advised to hire an angle grinder.

To cut by hand, measure the slab and mark the surface side with the edge of the bolster. Then turn the slab on its edge and make a nick in the edge both sides of the slab. You can afford to be a bit heavy-handed with this nick because the slab is unlikely to break. Turn the slab so that the back is facing you and you'll be able to mark the back by joining the two nicks.

Now lean the slab against your leg and start to tap a nick in the surface with the bolster. Turn it round and do the back, tapping fairly gently. Then tap the front again, and continue in this way until the slab cracks in half. The art lies in how hard you tap but it doesn't take too long to get used to it. It doesn't actually hurt your leg either, though it looks as though it should!

Our quadrant of paving proved a bit more difficult. Here, every one of the slabs at the edge had to be cut at an angle. Rather than face the frustration and expense of several broken slabs, we hired an angle grinder. This is a machine, generally electric, with a rotating disc at one end. The hire shop will stock special discs for cutting stone. When you go to hire the tool, make sure you also hire a pair of goggles and, if you haven't any, some strong gloves.

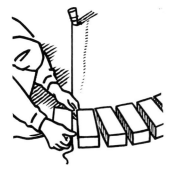

1. When putting in a brick trim, make sure all the bricks face into the centre of the circle.
2. They too, should be levelled to the nearest peg.

67

Do the cutting outside, because you'll create a very great deal of dust and possibly bits of grit. Then just mark the slab and cut to the mark with the disc. Since discs are quite expensive and don't last too long, it's best to cut a quarter of the way through on each side and then to tap the slab along the line of the cut with a club-hammer until it breaks. If the cut edge is going to be seen, though, as it might if the slab is on the front of a step for example, it's best to make a clean cut straight through from the surface side of the slab.

A brick trim

The edge of the paving can be made more attractive by installing a brick trim. If you do decide to do this, as we did, it's best to put it in first, before laying the paving. You must make sure you use special paving bricks since those used for wall-building will flake when they freeze. We chose the same blocks used for the circular feature (see pages 72–74).

If the edge of the paving is straight, laying out the brick edging is straightforward. But if it's circular like ours, you need to be careful to set the bricks not only in a perfect circle but also so that each brick is positioned so that it faces exactly into the centre of the circle.

When you marked out the quadrant, you will have done so with a cane at the centre and a piece of string (see page 23). The same set-up can be used to position the bricks, so make sure you leave the cane in. Tie a knot in the string at the required radius and line up each brick so that the knot is at the furthest end of the brick and the string runs exactly down

Keep off the paving for a few days to allow it to harden and then clean off any dried mortar. The quadrant shape here is ideal for a few chairs and a table outside the patio doors.

the centre. Then each brick can be set on a bed of mortar and tapped down to the correct level exactly as for laying paving slabs.

Planting pockets

So far, I have recommended butting the slabs up against each other and paving the whole area. This is the way it should normally be done for a patio or path which will receive constant use. But if you can leave spaces for plants here and there, in those parts of the patio that don't get so much use, the paved area takes on a much softer look.

Certainly you should leave out a few slabs near to the wall so that you can grow climbers up against it. And wherever you feel you won't actually be tripping over them, leave pockets for other plants in the main area too.

Of course, it would be too much of a fiddle to try to leave

The hardness of the paving can be softened by planting. Where you have left holes, cut through the concrete base and remove it and the soil beneath. Refill with good compost before planting.

areas of soil at exactly the right spot when you're putting down the base. So cover the whole area with the dry concrete mix and, once you've laid a bit of paving and left your hole for plants, chop out the concrete (not a difficult job with dry concrete), remove the soil as deeply as you can and replace with compost.

You'll need a well-drained mix for most plants, so use something like 3 parts good garden soil, 2 parts peat to 1 part coarse grit. Bear in mind that there's little plant food in this so you'll have to liquid feed from time to time.

Another way to soften the paving is to grow plants in the cracks between the slabs. There are many alpine plants that will thrive in this kind of situation, though you should avoid areas that will get a lot of wear. To leave space for plants, simply set the slabs slightly further apart and brush compost in between them. There's no need to hack out the concrete and indeed, this would be an impossible task. For alpines, there will be plenty of growing space between and under the slabs.

When you've filled up all the cracks, get a few packets of alpine seeds, mix them with sharp sand and just brush them across the paving. They'll fall down between the cracks and germinate without much difficulty.

For a list of plants suitable for growing in paving, see page 106.

Laying paving blocks
Several manufacturers now make paving blocks or brick paviors which will provide another interesting paving texture. There are two methods of laying them depending mainly on the area to be covered and, more important, the amount of weight the paving will have to bear. A garden path that will only be used to walk on can be laid by hand and tamped down with a club-hammer or a baulk of wood. If it's a driveway you intend to tackle, you'll have to pay more attention to the base and you'll need to hire a machine to tamp the blocks down.

Laying garden paths in blocks or paviors is actually great fun but there's a bit of work to do before laying can begin. Start by deciding on the width of the path by laying out a few blocks loose, just to ensure that your measurements are correct. Put them so that there's about a quarter of an inch (6 mm) between them and then make the width of the path equal to an exact number of blocks, so eliminating or at least dramatically reducing the amount of cutting necessary.

The blocks are laid on a bed of sharp sand, so the first necessity is to install an edge to the path to stop the sand drifting out. This can easily be done with wood and is made permanent by 'backing-up' with a fillet of concrete behind. Use 3 in × 1 in (8 cm × 2.5 cm) timber fixed to pegs driven into the ground at intervals. Make sure the pegs go *outside* the path area or they'll impede the blocks when you lay them. If you want to curve the path it helps to make a series of saw-cuts in the edging, on the inside of the curve. Make them about 2 inches (5 cm) apart and halfway through the wood and you'll find that bending becomes very much easier. Naturally the edgings should be levelled with a spirit-level as they are put in.

If your soil is firm and has been undisturbed, you may get away without a proper foundation. Much better put in at least a couple of inches (5 cm) though, just in case. Use dry ballast and cement as suggested for the patio base (page 64). Since you'll need 2 inches (5 cm) of sand plus the depth of the blocks (normally $2\frac{1}{4}$ inches (6 cm) you'll have to dig out about $6\frac{1}{4}$ inches (16 cm).

Put in the dry mix of ballast and cement and then cover that with sharp sand. You should wet it so that it's uniformly moist and then compact it well. Either use a garden roller or tread all over it. Afterwards rake it roughly level with a garden rake.

The final levelling is done with a notched board which you'll need to make. It should be a little wider than the path, with the notches cut at exactly path width and three quarters of an inch (2 cm) less than the depth of the block. So if the blocks are $2\frac{1}{4}$ inches (6 cm) thick, the notch should be $1\frac{1}{2}$ inches (4 cm) deep so that the sand will finish $1\frac{1}{2}$ inches (4 cm) below the level of the wooden edging. This will allow for the blocks settling three quarters of an inch (2 cm) when they're tamped down.

Lay out the first few rows of blocks as far as you can reach, bedding them down with a piece of wood and a club-hammer as you go. When you need to walk or kneel on the blocks you've laid, use a board across the whole width. If you need to cut blocks, you'll find it quite easy with a brick bolster.

When all the blocks are laid, cover the path with a shallow layer of sharp sand and brush it well into the cracks. If the blocks have not bedded down to the level of the top of the edging boards, you may have to go over the path with a plank

1. For block paving, the sand should be levelled with a notched board, using the shuttering for level.
2. Place the blocks in position and tap them down a little with the handle of a club-hammer.
3. Sweep fine sand between the blocks to hold them firm.
4. Put a board across and tamp down using a fencing post. More sand may then be needed.

and a baulk of wood tamping them down further.

If you lay the blocks in this way they may well settle a little further but this shouldn't matter. Settlement should be fairly uniform but the odd slight hollow here and there in fact adds something to the charm. There shouldn't be any problem with water lying on the surface since it will normally seep down between the blocks.

If you're laying a driveway, you'll have to take a lot more trouble. Here it's best to use precast concrete edgings, set in concrete, rather than relying on the wooden edging. When setting them, make sure you allow for a slope away from the house to remove excess water in wet weather.

The preparation also has to be more thorough. Here, the base should be at least 4 inches (10 cm) deep, preferably overlying a layer of rammed hardcore. It will help to lay the blocks in a herringbone fashion which forms a stronger bond, and they will have to be firmed with a machine. What you need is a flat-bed vibrator which you can hire from most small-tool hire shops. This will vibrate the blocks down very much firmer and there should be no problem of sinkage even if cars use the driveway.

Making a circular feature

Paving blocks laid in a circle make a very attractive feature and are not difficult to lay. Since the sunniest part of our garden was actually away from the house, we decided on a circular area of paving as a spot for sunbathing and as the main feature of the scheme. A wooden bench would make a pleasant sitting-out spot and a large, brightly planted urn would attract the eye across the garden to increase its apparent size.

Generally this kind of feature would be away from the house, so levels will depend upon the lie of the surrounding soil rather than on the damp-proof course. The method of laying the paving blocks is much the same as described for areas with straight edges, except that it's necessary to overcome the difficulty of making a circular edging.

Mark out the circle with a centre peg and a piece of string. Put pegs around the edge of the circle to mark the perimeter and also to set the levels. Before putting the pegs in, make a couple of marks on them. The first should be $1\frac{1}{2}$ inches (4 cm) from the top and the second $3\frac{1}{2}$ inches (9 cm) down. The centre peg should be tapped down so that the top finishes about 1 inch (2.5 cm) below the level of the surrounding soil. Level in the pegs round the edge so that they're about $\frac{1}{2}$ to 1 inch (13–25 mm) lower than the centre peg, to provide a fall.

Dig out sufficient soil to allow a 3-inch (8 cm) base of dry concrete which should reach the lowest mark on the pegs. This is tamped down hard as described before. Then cover with a 2-inch (5 cm) layer of sharp sand which should be consolidated and raked roughly level with the higher mark. Now remove the centre peg and replace it with one of the blocks. The top of this block should be level with the top of the sand.

Now you'll need some lengths of straight timber about $1\,\text{in} \times 1\frac{1}{2}\,\text{in}$ (2.5 cm × 4 cm). Roofing lathes are ideal for the purpose and they're stocked by any timber merchant. These are cut into about 3-foot (90 cm) lengths and set around the edge of the circle so that they are exactly level with the top marks on the pegs. Bed them in the sand and pack sand around them so that they won't move. Now, with a straight-edge resting on the centre block at one end, and on the roofing lathes at the other, you can scrape the sand level. In fact, if the area is anything but very small, this is really a two-person job.

Now put a wide board on the sand to work on, remove the

1. After digging out, pegging and laying the sand, bed some lathes into the sand at the correct level and pack more sand round them.
2. Remove the centre peg and replace with a stone block. The sand can then be levelled with a straight edge.
3. Starting in the middle, lay the blocks out on the sand in a series of circles. It's best to stand on a board.
4. When the circle is completed, put a flexible shuttering round the edge and secure with strong pegs.
5. Brush fine sharp sand into the spaces between the blocks. This will be worked down around the blocks to hold them firm.
6. Vibrate the blocks down with a flat-bed vibrator which can be hired quite easily. Then remove the shuttering and replace with concrete.

centre stone and replace the sand at the required level. Then set the stones in circular fashion. You'll see that you need special sizes for the centre part of the circle where the radius is small.

When all the stones are laid, put in the edging. This is made with 4-inch (10 cm) wide strips of $\frac{1}{8}$-inch (3 mm) plywood. They will easily bend around the stone circle and can be held in place with pegs. Don't skimp on the number of pegs you use or the plywood may belly outwards – one every 3 feet (90 cm) is the minimum. There's no need to worry about the levels of the edging this time, since it's only a temporary measure.

Now brush sharp sand into the joints and tamp the blocks down as before. Using a flat-bed vibrator is much to be preferred to hand tamping if the area is large.

The blocks should sink by about three quarters of an inch (2 cm) as before. After consolidating, remove the plywood edging and put a fillet of concrete around the edge to hold the sand permanently. This is made with 6 to 1 ballast and cement mixed fairly wet and trowelled down to leave it finishing at least 1 inch (2.5 cm) below the level of the blocks.

You may decide to install a circular block feature in an existing lawn. If you do, the turf will serve to retain the sand and there's no need for a concrete edging.

Building walls

This is a more difficult task than paving, needing a good eye and a fair amount of natural skill. Don't expect to emulate the brickies you have watched building the house. They were probably on piecework and going like a train! Take your time and stand back to cast a critical eye over your work quite often.

Choice of materials

Walls can be made out of brick or stone, but you must be careful in your choice. Above all, avoid materials that will flake in a hard frost. There are some bricks, like 'common flettons', for example, that are intended for inside walls only. They're cheap initially, but they'll last no more than a year or two. Ideally, use 'stock' bricks or at least 'sand-faced flettons' which are made for outdoor use. In fact, second-hand stock bricks can usually be bought from a demolition contractor at a fraction of the price of new ones and, because they are weathered, they look very attractive indeed.

As previously mentioned, it's a mistake to mix materials too much in a small garden. So if you're using paving slabs for a patio, make sure you buy the same kind of stone for the walling. Alternatively, you could match the brick of the house walls, as we did.

Foundations

For walls up to 3 feet (90 cm) high, the foundations should be twice the width of the wall and about 6 inches (15 cm) deep. Start by marking out the line of the proposed wall. If there are to be right-angles, mark them out carefully with a builder's square. Then dig a trench at least 8 inches (20 cm) deep and twice the width of the wall. Set some pegs at intervals along it and level them in with the spirit-level. The pegs should finish about 2 inches (5 cm) below soil level, so that none of the concrete will be seen.

The foundations should be made with a fairly dry but workable mix of ballast and cement at 6 parts to 1 and brought up to the top of the pegs. Tamp it down firmly as you go, to eliminate air pockets. Then leave it to harden for several days before setting the bricks or stone blocks.

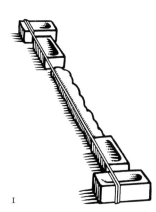

1

2

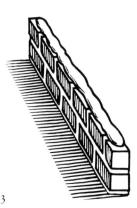

3

1. Start by setting the two end bricks and run a tight line along the top edge of the bricks.
2. The line will help align the rest of the bricks in that course. 'Butter' the ends with mortar before laying.
3. As successive courses are laid, the bricks must be 'bonded' for extra strength.

If the wall runs in two directions both runs must be put up together so that they are bonded at the corners.

Laying the walling

Start by mixing up the mortar, using 3 parts builders' sand to 1 part of masonry cement. This is a slightly more flexible cement than Portland cement and will prevent cracking when the wall expands and contracts as temperatures alter. The mix should be quite sloppy if you're laying bricks, but drier for stone. It's easier to lay bricks with fairly wet mortar; while any excess which falls onto the face of a brick wall will easily scrape off the smooth surface, it sticks to the rougher face of stone and stains it.

Set the two ends of the wall first by putting down a shallow layer of mortar and tapping the block into it. Use either the blade of the trowel for bricks or the handle of a club-hammer if you're laying stone on drier mortar.

Now you need to run a bricklayer's line along the front edge of the bricks. I find the easiest way is to wrap it several times round a spare brick to hold it down each end. Put the line on top of the brick and hold it there with another spare brick rested on top. You may well find you need to move the bricks you've already laid, just to line them up exactly.

It's worth taking a lot of time and trouble over the end-bricks because they set the line and level for all the rest. Once the line is in position and nice and tight, you can then lay the rest of the course quite quickly. The line will give you the correct line and level, though it's worth checking for level both ways with the spirit-level every now and then, just to make sure.

Lay the whole line of mortar out now, and start placing the walling. If you're laying bricks, you'll find it quite easy to 'butter' one end with mortar before you lay each one. It can then be pushed up tight against the last one you laid, forming an instant mortar joint between the two. If you're laying stone blocks, you won't be able to do that. With drier mortar, it's difficult to get it to stick, so in this case simply set the block half an inch (13 mm) away from the last block and point in with mortar after you've laid the whole row.

The mortar joints must be staggered to give strength and to look right. This means that if you're building a straight run of wall you'll have to start off every other course with half a brick. It's easy to cut them with a brick bolster and a hammer.

If the wall runs in two directions, you'll have a corner which will obviate the need for cutting bricks in half. The illustration opposite shows clearly why.

Some manufacturers supply 'jumpers' with their stone walling. These are stones twice the thickness of the rest which can be used here and there to good effect to give a 'random' look to the wall. Obviously, if you have a jumper in a course, it will push the line out of true, so just leave a space for it when you come to it and set it when the rest of the course is laid.

As you progress upwards, there is a great danger of allowing the wall to lean. It's not difficult to check a brick wall with the spirit-level put vertically on the smooth face of the wall. But stone walls with a rough face are more difficult.

Make sure you check each stone with the spirit-level *across* the run of the wall to avoid tilting and, every now and then, pause for a while, go to the end of the wall and squint down it to make sure it *looks* level. With stone walling, that's about all you can do. If you're worried that your eye is not too good, you can help yourself with a sighting post. Bang a post in near the end of the wall and level that with the spirit-level so that it's exactly upright. Then you can compare it with the line of the wall when you squint down it, and you should be able to get it dead level.

When the mortar is dry but not hard, you'll need to rake out the joints on the front of the wall, to slightly recess them. I use a small piece of wood for this job, cut to just less than half an inch (13 mm) and rounded at the end to give a neat recessed joint. When the raking out is complete, brush over the whole of the front of the wall with a soft brush to remove any excess mortar that may have stuck.

If you're building a double wall, it's a good idea to bond the two parts together for strength. Do this with a builder's 'butterfly' – a piece of wire bent to the shape of a pair of wings, which is bedded at intervals into the mortar of both walls.

If your wall is intended to retain soil, it's very important to remember to include drainage holes at the bottom. Otherwise water will build up behind the wall and, with nowhere to go, it could push the whole thing down. Just leave out half a block at about 6-foot (2 m) intervals in the bottom course.

The tops of walls must be finished off with a coping. This is particularly important with brick walls because it prevents water being absorbed by the soft brick. If that happens, the bricks will flake in a hard frost. In fact, all walls, stone or brick, look much better with a coping, so it's worth doing in any case.

Manufacturers of walling stone always supply a special coping, made to just the right size for the job. It should overlap the front of the walling by about 1 inch (2.5 cm).

If you're building a single brick wall only 4½ inches (11 cm) thick, you'll need to use a similar type of stone or precast concrete coping. In our garden we used the same paving slabs used for the paved areas, simply cut into 6-inch (15 cm) strips with the angle grinder. If the wall is low, this makes an ideal place to sit too. If your wall is double thickness you could, alternatively, use 9-inch (23 cm) bricks laid on edge.

Steps

Once you've mastered the technique for paving and walling, stone steps are not difficult because they're just a combination of the two. The walling is used for the 'risers' and the paving slabs for the steps themselves.

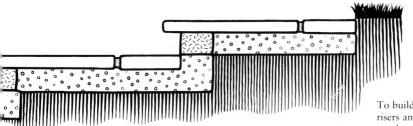

To build steps, use walling for the risers and paving slabs for the treads.

Decide first of all, the number and width of the steps. Check the height overall, using a straight-edge and spirit-level from the top of the slope as suggested for fencing (see page 49). The height of the risers can vary a little but you must be careful not to make steps dangerous. If the risers are too low, you'll create a series of 'trips' and you'll find your guests who are not used to them falling up them! On the other hand, risers that are too high are difficult to negotiate for some folk, especially older people and small children. About 5 to 7 inches (13–18 cm) is ideal.

When building the steps, always start at the bottom and, if they run onto the lawn, remember that the lowest tread should consist of a paving slab set into the lawn just about 1 inch (2.5 cm) below the turf level. That way you'll be able to run the mower over it without damage.

Put a 6-inch (15 cm) foundation behind the first tread and build a single wall on it. Then dig out behind to the required levels, fill in with a base of dry ballast and lay the paving treads. The front of the slabs should overlap the walling by about 1 inch (2.5 cm), and in this case, of course, there should be a continuous bed of mortar on the walling side, rather than the customary five mounds.

Then put another foundation behind the slabs and build the next riser. Note that you should never build the riser on top of the paving slab. In the case of even slight sinkage, that would tip the slab, making the steps very dangerous indeed.

Wooden steps

In an informal setting, wooden steps look very attractive and are much easier and cheaper to build. The risers can be made with either old railway sleepers (you'll find ads for them in the farming magazines), or chunks of logs. Either can be fixed by driving in a strong stake behind them at each end and nailing through.

The 'treads' are simply cut out of the soil and can be made attractive and mud-free with a thick layer of ornamental bark chips. You'll find those in various grades at the garden centre.

Opposite. A good lawn makes a fine foreground for the mixed border.

LAWNS

Britain has just about the best climate in the world for growing grass. All that rain does do us a *bit* of good really! So it's perhaps for this reason that the lawn is such a popular part of most English gardens.

Certainly a well-kept lawn does set off the garden well. It's the perfect foreground for flower borders and it makes a first-class surface for recreation and relaxation. If you have small children it does away with any worries about them injuring themselves when they fall over and, if you happen to be a sporty type, it's the ideal place for games like bowls or badminton, or for sharpening up your putting!

Mind you, our lawns are expected to put up with quite a lot of abuse. Lawn grass must be about the only plant in the world that's walked on regularly and also hard-pruned every week of the growing season and yet is still expected to look marvellous all the time. The amazing thing is that it will! But only if you start out on the right foot and you subsequently treat it well. When you think about it, it jolly well deserves a bit of extra tender loving care.

Preparation

Whether you decide you want the finest of fine show lawns or simply an area that will take some hard wear, whether you intend to sow it or turf it, the preparation is exactly the same.

There is a school of thought that claims that the preparation for turf need not be as thorough as for a seeded lawn, but that's just wishful thinking I'm afraid. The only way is the right way.

The first indication of what will be necessary will come when you dig that initial hole to find out about your soil (see page 35). If you come across the hard layer I've already warned about, you'll have to break it up. Leave it and your lawn will always be a soggy mess and the grass will never look happy. Even grass doesn't like to have wet feet.

Drainage

Once the layer is broken and drainage restored, you'll be able to assess the need for further measures. If the soil is heavy and still lies very wet, it will pay to do something about extra drainage. But that, I'm afraid, is not quite so easy as it sounds.

You'll read, in several books, instructions to lay drainage tiles to take away the excess water. Trouble is, where do you take it to? If you just divert it into the next-door garden you're likely to get something more than the odd black look, and if you dig a soak-away, as is sometimes suggested, you're still likely to get trouble. Bad drainage is caused by an impermeable subsoil, so the soakaway is going to be no better drained than the rest of the garden. Once it's filled with water, you're right back to square one!

Sometimes the local council will allow you to run garden drains into the storm drains, but you *must* ask them first. Even so, they will expect an expert job of linking them in and they'll probably send down an inspector to make sure it's up to standard, so you may well have to contract out that end of the job.

Of course, if you're lucky enough to have a ditch passing your door, then there's no problem, but that's pretty unlikely. However, there's normally no need to go to extraordinary lengths.

Grass doesn't need a very deep soil to grow perfectly well, so it is possible to improve the upper layer just enough to make the top few inches acceptable to the grass. Some football clubs have actually laid their pitches on pure sand and they're growing very well indeed. And your lawn is unlikely to get that kind of wear!

The answer is to work into the soil a good dressing of coarse grit. Don't use sharp sand because on some soils that can do more harm than good, and *never* use builders' sand.

How much you use will, of course, depend on how heavy the soil is. Generally a barrow-load every 2 to 3 square yards will do.

That should be enough to make most soils acceptable to grass but, in very severe cases, it may be worth going one step further. If the land is still really boggy, you should put a 3-inch (8 cm) layer of coarse weathered ash (power stations can generally help) or coarse grit over the whole area and then cover that with a further 3 inches (8 cm) of topsoil. That will raise the level of the lawn above the boggy area and will give excellent results. Naturally it has the disadvantage that it's expensive and a lot of extra work. But conditions would have to be really extreme to necessitate going to those lengths.

If the soil is very light, the reverse treatment is necessary. Now you'll need something in it to help retain as much moisture as possible.

Any organic material will do. Ideally dig in farmyard manure or well-rotted stable manure. Spent mushroom compost is excellent and generally quite cheap or, if you really can't find any of the cheaper materials, you'll have to do it the expensive way and use peat.

Of course, any organic material will eventually rot down in the soil and disappear. And under a lawn, it's not easy to replace because you have to get it below the level of the grass. So you may like to consider using one of the more permanent materials – perlite or vermiculite. These are minerals that have been expanded with heat to form porous particles. Both hold many times their own weight of water and will improve drainage and aeration at the same time.

I must say that I couldn't recommend using either for digging into the borders, for the simple reason that they're somewhat obtrusive. Vermiculite is a shiny fawn colour while perlite is glaringly brilliant white. Neither improve the look of the soil. But of course, underneath the lawn they won't be seen, and they'll certainly do a remarkably good job, virtually for ever.

Sloping gardens
If your garden is on a steep slope, you may consider terracing the lawn into a series of levels. This can look very attractive and should greatly increase the interest of the garden. But it's not quite as straightforward as it may seem. It isn't good enough simply to remove the topsoil from the upper part of the slope and transfer it to the lower half to level it off. That

way, unless your topsoil is very deep, you're likely to leave the top part with only a very thin layer of topsoil over the subsoil.

Instead, the topsoil must be stripped off completely, the subsoil levelled and the topsoil replaced. It seems like an awful lot of work, but it's quite necessary I'm afraid.

Cultivation

Normally it's only necessary to single-dig the lawn area, working the organic matter into the bottom of each trench as you go.

If your garden is big, it's worth considering hiring a mechanical cultivator. This is also a good idea if your house is one of a row of new properties and the fences have not been erected. If you can get your new neighbours to club together you could almost certainly do the whole lot in a day, so it won't be expensive.

If you've had to double-dig the area to break up a solid layer, it's important now to leave it for a while to settle (it's also a very good excuse for a rest!). It depends a lot on the weather, but ideally you should allow at least 3 to 4 weeks. This could also give you the opportunity of creating what the old gardeners called a 'stale seed-bed'. I've no idea why it's called that, but it's a very useful technique.

Digging will have brought a lot of weed seeds to the surface where they'll germinate and compete with the grass seed, so the idea is to forestall them. Leave the land untouched until the weed seeds germinate and then, while they're still small, hoe them off and sow your grass. That will have dealt with the first flush so your grass will have a chance to get growing before any weeds that are blown in afterwards can germinate. It will also have allowed the soil to settle a bit more and, if the weed seeds germinate, you'll know that the soil is warm enough for the grass seed too.

Levelling

Lawns need not necessarily be dead flat. In fact, a certain amount of undulation in a bigger lawn adds a lot of interest. However, it's vital to make the undulations gentle and rolling so a lot will depend on the size of the area to be grassed. Obviously, the first consideration must be ease of cutting, so smaller areas may have to remain flat.

It's most important, when preparing the lawn for sowing or turfing, to eliminate any local bumps and dents. Small, low

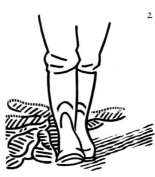

1. To prepare the soil for seed or turf, start by roughly levelling with the back of a fork.
2. It's essential to consolidate the soil and the only way is by treading.
3. The difficult part is the final raking level. Take time and trouble.

areas will be missed by the mower which will simply ride over the top. That means that the grass in that spot will become rank and coarse and the lawn will look patchy. But even if you level the lawn perfectly before sowing, it will still settle unevenly unless it is uniformly consolidated all over *before* the final levelling.

Start by roughly levelling the whole area with the back of a fork. Don't worry too much about local levels at this stage but make sure the level is generally as you want it. Then it must be evenly consolidated.

The last tool you want for this job is the garden roller. The effect of this is to push down the high bits and ride over the low areas. These will then sink further, making the lawn even more uneven than it was before. The only way to do it is with your feet. But here you may have yet another excuse for a day off, because you'll do more harm than good treading over the soil when it's wet. That breaks down the structure, destroying the drainage and rendering it airless. The rule is never to work the soil if it's wet enough to stick to your boots. Ideally, the top should be dry and crumbly.

Working systematically up and down, tread over every square inch with your weight on your heels. There's no doubt that this is an arduous task but one of the most important in the whole operation.

Before doing the final raking down, it's a good idea to scatter a little fertiliser over the area. This enables you to rake it into the surface whilst doing the final levelling and it means that the fertiliser will be dissolved and available to the young

grass seedlings right from the start. Use Growmore applied at about a handful to each square yard. There's no need to be too accurate at that low level, but make sure you don't overdo it or you could cause scorching of the young roots.

Now comes the delicate operation of final levelling. Of course, you can't learn the technique from a book. It's a matter of a good eye, a fine touch and a bit of practice. But there are a few points to note.

First of all, work just a little way in front of your feet, keeping the head of the rake almost horizontal to the ground. Don't stretch a long way forward and drag the soil towards you or you'll tend to pull it into ridges. It also pays, every now and then, to stand back from the work, crouch down and squint across the surface with your head as low as possible. That way, high and low spots show up much better.

If your soil is very stony, you'll find it's quite hard work pulling a pile of stones along all the time. So have a barrow handy and just shovel the piles off from time to time.

Turf or seed?

The choice between the two methods of making a lawn is generally made for you in your first garden – by the bank manager! Turf is considerably more expensive though it does, of course, have the great advantage of immediacy. You can use a turf lawn laid in spring or summer within about six weeks of laying – a little longer with autumn or winter laying. A spring-sown lawn is usable within about 10 weeks and an autumn-sown one not until well into the following spring. When I say 'usable' I mean you can walk on it. Hard wear should wait for six months, regardless of the method of making the lawn.

Of course, there's turf and turf and you need to be very careful about how you buy it. Alas, the turf industry is renowned for having more than its fair share of 'cowboys' and this makes it very difficult for the reputable traders. Of course it is possible to buy excellent turf advertised as 'parkland turf' but unfortunately that label seems to cover a multitude of different products.

The reputable turf grower will buy a field from a farmer, mow it, weed treat it, rake it, roll it and feed it for about a year or even two. Then the turf is well worth having.

The cowboy buys a field and immediately cuts the turf, often with no treatment whatsoever. That often means that you're buying nothing more or less than cow-pasture. I've even seen it come complete with cow-pats! Often it's infested with weeds, what grass there is is coarse and tough and, because no rolling has gone on to flatten it out before cutting, the uneven ground produces turves that are thick one end and thin the other, and may be full of holes.

So try to see the turf before you buy. Sometimes this is claimed to be impossible for obvious reasons so, whatever you do, stress when you order that you want excellent quality and that if the turf is poor you won't accept delivery. But better still, spend about three times as much and buy 'cultivated turf'.

Now this really is the best quality you can buy and, if it means pawning the cat, it's well worth it! Here the grower buys a field and ploughs in the existing grass. He then carefully levels, fertilises and sows a selected lawn-grass seed. Then, during the next couple of years, he rolls it, mows it, weed treats and feeds it just as if it were Gleneagles.

The turf you get as a result is *only* top-quality grass with not a weed in sight. It's green and healthy and each turf is cut to an exact thickness all over, making it a pleasure to lay. You can even choose whether you have a hard-wearing mixture of grasses or a super-fine one, though bear in mind here that the fine turf is not necessarily the best bet. Only choose it if you can give it a lot of time, trouble and expense in the future.

Starting with seed will give you all these advantages too, at a fraction of the cost. The only disadvantage, really, is that it takes longer to establish.

When choosing grass seed, think carefully about the conditions you can give it. These days, though it's virtually impossible to buy your own specified mixture made up especially for you, there are plenty of different ready-mixed blends available.

First of all, consider the aspect. If your garden, or even part of it, is in heavy shade, ordinary grass-seed mixtures will not do. You must buy a mix made up specially for shady areas. You may have a mixture of conditions where you intend to grow grass – for example, a sunny, open spot surrounded by trees. Well, you'll just have to sow the two areas separately with two different mixtures. What's more, you'll need to cut the grass in the shady area less frequently.

Think about the kind of wear the grass will get. If you have two or three boisterous children who want to kick a ball about, you'll *have* to settle for a hard-wearing mixture, but if it's just normal wear, a finer grass will thrive.

But above all, consider the amount of subsequent management you can give the lawn. Really fine lawns do need a lot of maintenance and a fair bit of money spent on them. And, if they don't get it, they'll sulk and eventually revert back to coarser grasses.

My advice would be to buy a first-quality mixture containing no perennial rye-grass *only* if you are prepared to cut the lawn with a cylinder mower at least twice a week and preferably more, feed it twice a year, rake it, water it and weed treat it as necessary, and to use it just for gentle walking on. If you can't, the best bet in my view is to buy one of the newer strains of perennial rye-grass that have been bred especially for lawns. There are a few about. Perennial rye-grass has a bad reputation because the early breeding was done for cattle feeding and not for lawns. New varieties are shorter, much finer and very hard-wearing.

Sowing

The spring and the autumn are generally considered the best times to sow grass seed. I must say that I've done it every month from April to October with no ill effect and I wouldn't hesitate to sow during that period provided the weather is with you.

Whether you're sowing seed or laying turf, it's a good idea to give it a flying start with a dressing of fertiliser.

Naturally you wouldn't sow when the soil is soaking wet nor when it's bone dry. The ideal time is when the top has just dried out after a soaking. Then the seed will germinate quickly and once it's through you'll be able to water if the weather turns dry. Try to avoid watering before germination because this has two ill effects. First, it tends to 'cap' the soil, forming a hard crust on the top which the seedlings have a difficult time breaking through. Secondly, it washes the seed into the lowest spots, so you'll get overcrowding in some places and sparse germination in others.

It's recommended that grass seed should be sown at the rate of 2 oz per square yard (60 g/sq. m) but in my view that's a mite excessive. In fact I would go as far as cutting that rate in half and sowing only 1 oz (30 g). So, when you're buying, measure up the area in square yards (sq. m) and buy 1 oz (30 g) for each.

Start by marking out the area to be sown. The best way is to set out a number of canes to mark the edges, but don't worry at this stage about being absolutely accurate. You'll have a better chance to get the edges right when you come to cut them out once the seed has established itself.

I don't believe it's necessary to go to all the lengths of measuring out square yards (sq. m) with strings and canes

To avoid disturbing the levels again, the best tool to rake in the seed is a spring-tine lawn rake.

and weighing out the seed. Simply stand with your legs stretched fairly widely apart. That should be roughly a yard (metre). Then lean forward as far as you can without tipping over and scatter a couple of handfuls of seed in that area. You won't be far out. Even if the distribution of the seed is not as even as you would have liked, it will spread out evenly when you rake it in.

Alternatively, if you want to be a little more accurate, measure out 1 square yard (1 sq. m) and weigh up 1 oz (30 g) of seed to scatter over it. When you've seen what that looks like, you'll be able to judge by eye near enough.

When you're sowing, don't worry too much about restricting the seed exactly to the area you have marked out. It's best to go over the edges a little to ensure that you get a good 'take' of grass there to give you a good firm edge to cut later.

The best tool for raking the seed in is a spring-tine rake. If you haven't got one, it's worth buying because you'll certainly need it later. Aim to cover about half the seed. You'll find that this rake doesn't disturb the levels so much as the garden rake you used for the levelling.

Afterwards, there's no need to roll the lawn. Though this is sometimes recommended, it can have the effect of creating a hard crust on the surface of the soil, slowing down or even preventing germination.

After sowing grass seed, the word will quickly spread round the bird population that you offer the best free dinner in town and they'll descend upon you in droves. In fact, although it raises the blood pressure somewhat because whenever you look out of the window the garden is covered with hungry birds a-pecking, they rarely take more than their share. Nonetheless, it's perhaps worth protecting it for a while.

A bit of netting laid over the surface will generally do, or you can put a few short sticks around the area and stretch black cotton between them.

But the way I like best is with polythene. You can use ordinary clear sheeting, but you'll have to be pretty vigilant if you do. Just as soon as you see the first blade of green you'll have to whip it off. I much prefer the perforated sheeting which is sold in garden centres as 'floating cloche'. This is simply clear polythene with thousands of holes in it which serve to provide some ventilation so that the sheeting can be left on for longer without harm.

The great thing about polythene is that not only does it do a one hundred per cent job of cheating the birds of their free nosh, it also speeds up germination considerably. That grass will be through and growing before you can curse a sparrow!

Laying turf

Turfing can be done at any time of the year providing that the soil is in good enough condition. You can happily put it down in the middle of winter, except when the soil is frozen solid (when you wouldn't get the turf anyway), or when it's under a covering of snow. Unlike seed sowing, your timing is not really dependent on the soil temperature. Mind you, it'll take a bit longer to root in winter and if you choose the driest spell in the middle of summer, you'll have to water regularly, so it's best to choose your time if you can. Ideally, that's from the beginning of March to the end of May and the end of August to the beginning of January.

Order your turf by the square yard or metre and, when it arrives, stack it as near to the site as you can. You should be all ready to lay it then, because it won't want to be stacked rolled up for too long. Without light it will turn yellow in a couple of days in summer. At the same time, you should have to hand a good strong wheelbarrow to take the turves round to the back of the house, a few wide boards (scaffold planks can be hired and are ideal), a rake and an old knife. You'll also need a lawn sprinkler and a hose, especially if you're laying the turves in the summer.

There's no point in laying turf on soil that's bone dry, so if you're laying it in the summer and have had to wait for it to arrive, you may need to water first. Try to think ahead and put the sprinkler on for a couple of hours or so a day or two before turfing.

Start by laying out any curved edges. It's much easier to do it this way than to try to cut an edge later. If you lay out that edge, you can push and pull the turves into line with the rake and you can have a good look from time to time to make quite sure the curve suits your eye. It's surprising that what looks good on paper can sometimes appear quite out of place on the ground. And remember the golden rule – if it looks right, it *is* right.

When the edge is in position, just tap the turves down to get them in firm contact with the soil and to stop them moving about.

Now begin the turfing proper, starting preferably from a straight edge. Lay out the first row of turves and pull the ends of each turf into the one you've just laid, using the back of

1. When laying out the turves, always work off boards to avoid spoiling the levels.

2. Pull each turf into the previously laid one, using the back of the rake.

3. Tamp the turves down with the back of the rake to ensure good contact with the soil.

4. At the end of each row, lay the turf over the edging turf and cut off the excess.

the rake. Try not to stretch the turves when laying them out because they're likely to shrink back to size, leaving ugly gaps between.

Then tap down each turf with the back of the rake. If you've levelled the ground properly to start with, you won't need to bash them down with a rammer as is sometimes recommended. Just a gentle tap to put them into intimate contact with the soil is all that's needed.

Now put one of your scaffold boards on the turf you've laid. You should make sure you never tread either on the turf or on the soil you're about to put it on. That way you make indentations with your feet and ruin all the hard work you did at the levelling stage. I find it's worth putting out two rows of boards plus a line to get you from the edge of the lawn over to the boards.

The second row of turves can now be put out. Most books

will tell you to bond turves like bricks in a wall, but this is absolutely unnecessary. If your borders are curved you'll do that automatically anyway, and even if they're not I can see no point in it at all. What you should do is again to pull the edges of the second row into the first with the back of the rake and then tamp down the whole row.

When you get to the end of each row you'll find that you need to cut the turf to fit. Simply lay the end of the turf over the edging turf you've already laid and cut off the excess.

You may find that you can almost, but not quite, reach the end of the row with the last turf. In that case, lay it out and use a bit of one of the scraps you've cut off to fill in.

However good the turf may be, you're bound to find that from time to time there's either a very thin spot or even a hole. This is often because there has been a stone underneath the turf just at the level of the cutter.

In the case of thin patches, they are best cut right out and the two bits of turf simply moved up together to fill the hole. If you come across a hole in the turf, just tear a piece off one of the scraps and stuff it in. It'll grow, however small it is, and, within a couple of days, you won't be able to see where it was.

After a few weeks the turf will have rooted. The first mowing should be with the cutters set as high as possible.

When you've finished, take the boards off and get the sprinkler going. The weather doesn't have to be very dry or hot for the turves to start shrinking, so you can expect to need water right from the start. The only exception would be for turf laid in the winter or, of course, during rainy weather in spring or summer. But, in my experience, it *never* rains just as you've laid turf. That would be just too convenient!

The length of time taken for the turf to root will vary from about three days to three weeks depending on the weather. During that time it's vital to water regularly. Bear in mind that the only way the grass can get water is through you, and without it cracks will rapidly appear between the turves. If that happens, the only remedy is to brush a top-dressing between the turves to fill in the spaces. That's an awful lot of work and it looks *terrible*. So make sure the sprinkler goes round the lawn, leaving it on for no more than about half an hour at a time.

Until it has rooted, the turf does look a bit sorry for itself. The grass lies flat and has a bluish appearance. However, you'll soon see when it has managed to push out some roots, because it perks up noticeably. The grass starts to stand up and looks a fresh green again.

Immediate aftercare
Neither seeded nor turfed lawns should be cut until the grass is about 2 inches (5 cm) tall. The best thing to do then with a turfed lawn is to roll it by running the mower over it with the cutters held clear of the grass. If your mower is one of the light electric models you won't be able to do that, so try to borrow or even hire a light roller.

Then, after two days, cut the grass, first lifting the mower's cutters to their highest point. This will just top the grass and is sufficient for the first cut. For the second one, lower the cutters a little and put them lower still over the subsequent couple of cuts. This may seem like an awful nuisance, especially when you have to adjust the cutters with spanners. But, if you want to see the reason, just cut a bit of long grass very short. The result is a very yellow lawn which eventually turns an unhealthy-looking greenish-white. It will certainly recover after a few days but is a symptom of the harm done to the grass. In fact, you should also raise the cutters at the beginning of every season when the grass is long, even when the lawn is well established.

The final adjustment should leave the grass about half an

inch (13 mm) long. It's never a good thing to cut it too short, since this tends to encourage bare patches which are later colonised by moss and weeds.

A seeded lawn is treated in much the same way. Here, though, it's a good idea to go over it before the first cut, bucket in hand, removing any large stones that may have worked their way to the surface. They could cause untold damage to the mower and can, in fact, be quite dangerous.

Then try to roll it as before. This is even more desirable on a seeded lawn for two reasons. First, the roller will press down any stones too small to hand-pick. Secondly, and even more important, it will also bruise the young stems and encourage them to 'tiller'. This is really much the same process as pinching out the top of a plant to make it grow bushier. There are several small growth buds at the base of each grass stalk which will be encouraged to grow out rapidly when the stalk itself is bruised. So what will look like a very thin lawn at first, because it consists of a series of single-leafed plants, will quickly thicken up as each single leaf becomes a clump.

Despite starting with a 'stale seed-bed', you're quite likely to find several weeds thriving amongst the grass too. Well, you can forget most of them. Many will be annuals which will simply die out when you cut their tops off with the mower. A few may be perennials but most of those will be taller-growing plants, which again will not be able to survive regular cutting.

There may be one or two 'rosetted' weeds that grow close to the ground, like dandelions, buttercups or daisies. Because the mower misses them, they won't succumb. If you spot these, try first to pull them out. If you can't, either cut them off with a knife, or drop a tiny pinch of table salt right into the middle of the plant. Don't get any on the grass though, because it will kill that too. It's not a good idea to use weed-killers on young grass.

Feeding should not be necessary in the first year either. Leave that until the following spring and then use either Growmore or, for a rapid green-up, a proprietary lawn fer-tiliser.

A turfed lawn will already have a well-defined edge, though you will need to cut it a little deeper with a spade or edging iron later on when it has made good roots.

The edge of a seeded lawn will need cutting out afterwards. Don't be too impatient to do this job. It's important to allow the grass to make a good fibrous root system so that the edge is firm. It should be possible to cut the edges after about two months, but by this time the grass will have grown quite high because you won't have been able to get the mower over it right at the edges. Don't throw the clumps of grass away, but dig them in to the borders where the grass will help improve the soil structure.

All you need do during the first season is to cut the grass at least once a week, putting the cuttings on the compost heap, of course. Keep the sprinkler going round in dry weather and cut the edges with a pair of long-handled shears about every fourth cut.

GARDEN FEATURES

When you plan your garden, you're likely to want to include some kind of focal point – a feature around which the rest of the garden revolves. Or you may prefer to add it later. It could be an area to grow favourite plants, like a raised bed for acid-lovers or a scree-garden for alpines. You may want to liven up the garden with a pool or to add a barbecue for those alfresco parties.

What you must do is to ensure that it doesn't 'take over'. It's all too easy to get carried away and allow a hobby horse to grow out of all proportion so that it dominates the whole garden. Obviously, the best way to get it in scale is to plan it right from the outset, but that's simply not how most gardens work.

Most of us find that, once the garden's built, there's a bit of a gap in our weekends and we look around for something else to add or some existing feature to improve. Half the fun of gardening is that your plot will be continually evolving. You never really finish.

So it's not a bad idea to plan the feature on paper first and then to stick a few canes in the garden and walk around them a few times trying to visualise what the completed thing will look like. It always pays in this job to take your time.

Pools

Moving water has a special attraction in the garden. It adds life and provides a home for a whole new range of plants that will not survive without water. And it will become a drinking fountain for all kinds of wildlife. In fact I would say that if you decide to garden your plot entirely organically, forgoing all chemical pesticides and fertilisers, a pool is essential. For then you'll need to attract birds and insect predators into your garden to keep the pests down. And a garden pool is a sure-fire way to do it.

But there's one very important factor to take into consideration before you start. If you have small children, your pool could be a death-trap. Yes, I know that sounds melodramatic, but small kids *have* been drowned in garden pools, even those only a few inches deep. If you must have both moving water and children, there is a way round it which I'll cover later.

If you just want to provide a water-hole for birds and insects (and perhaps the odd small mammal), and your garden is small, you can make an attractive pool with half a wooden barrel. You can buy them at most garden centres these days. You may have to settle for one with holes in the bottom, since most are sold for plant containers. If so, buy a short length of dowelling of exactly the right size and just hammer a bit in to fill the hole. Don't glue it or paint it because that may stop it swelling when it gets wet.

You'll probably find that the whole barrel will leak like a sieve at first. That's because it has been allowed to dry out, but a good soaking will soon put matters right. Just keep filling it up with water and it will eventually become completely leak-proof.

It's essential to sink it in the ground. Small pools always go green in the summer because the water heats up quickly. If you bury the pool, it keeps it cool and it will stay as clear as a bell.

When it's in, set it exactly level either with a spirit-level or just by filling it with water to the top. Firm the soil back around it and the job is almost done.

You will need to plant with oxygenating weed, which is just planted in an inch (2.5 cm) of heavy soil at the bottom. I would also put in some fairy moss (*Azolla caroliniana*) to float on the top, and rest a couple of potted marginal plants, like irises or the sweet flag (*Acorus calamus*), on a brick or two at the edge so that the water just covers their roots.

You would even have room for a water-lily if you stick to one of the miniatures like *Nymphaea candida* or *N. laydekeri* 'Purpurata'. Ghastly Latin names, I know, but a good aquatic plant centre will be able to translate!

If you have small children, you could use the tub for a 'drown-proof' pool. Fit a small submersible pump in the bottom of the tub so that the top of the outlet pipe reaches just above the top of the barrel. Surround it with a few bricks and then pile some large cobbles around and on top of it. The top of the cobbles should be about level with the top of the tub.

If the pump has a spray nozzle on top, remove it and then fill the tub with water. Enough will get into it between the cobbles to allow the pump to bubble up a little jet of water over the cobbles. It sounds soothing and it looks good, without the slightest risk to your children.

You may wish to make a full-sized pool as the main feature

in the garden and there's no doubt that it does add a lot of interest. It makes a real haven for all kinds of wildlife, from scudding water-boatmen to shimmering dragonflies. Where they come from always seems a mystery to me, but come they certainly do. By begging a little spawn from a neighbour with a pool, you could also introduce frogs. And they'll more or less solve your slug problem for you too.

An informal pool set in the grass is not difficult. Start by digging out a hole roughly like the drawing. You may not want to include a bog-garden area, in which case you simply make the left-hand side the same as the right. But I do urge you to fit in the bog-garden if you can, because it allows you to grow some wonderful plants you would otherwise find very difficult. Just take a look at a stand of candelabra primulas in the spring and you'll see what I mean!

It's essential to make the edges of the hole absolutely level all the way round. Otherwise you'll get large areas of the liner showing above the waterline. So, the first job is to set some level pegs all round the pool edge, levelling them exactly with the spirit-level.

The hole is lined with a waterproof butyl-rubber sheet but first you must guard against sharp stones working upwards to puncture it later. You can do this by lining the hole with a 2-inch (5 cm) layer of builders' sand pressed into the surface or, better still, with a special fibre sheet. You can buy this material at the aquatic specialists when you buy the liner.

When the sheet is in position, place the liner over the hole and weigh the edges down with a few bricks. Then simply fill

If you use a liner, making a pool is a simple and relatively inexpensive affair. This cross-section shows the various levels required for a pool designed to attract wildlife and to incorporate a wet area to grow bog plants.

1. It's easy to make a pool from half a barrel. Start by sinking it into the ground.
2. It's essential to level it both ways so that the water comes level with the top all round.
3. Put a layer of heavy soil in the bottom, fill it with water and plant it up.

up with water. The weight of the water will gradually force the liner to the bottom of the hole, stretching it into place. You will have to go round folding it here and there as it fills, to make a neat job.

You may find, when the water reaches the top, that you have not been quite accurate with your levelling and the edge of the pool is lower at one point than another. In that case, simply lift the edge of the liner, push more soil underneath and pat it down.

When the liner is in place and finally levelled, the excess can be cut off, leaving an edge of about 6 inches (15 cm). Rake about 3 inches (8 cm) of soil over the top of this overlap and finally hold it down with turf.

The bottom of the pool is filled with a 3-inch (8 cm) layer of heavy garden soil. It naturally makes the pool look like an ugly mud-hole at first, but it will settle in about 24 hours to leave the water reasonably clear. On the shallow side of the pool, make a sloping beach of large pebbles. Birds and small mammals find this invaluable when they come down for a drink. The bog-garden area is then filled right to the top with soil and the pool's ready for planting.

Plants for the pool

Your best plan when choosing plants is to get a catalogue from an aquatic specialist. There are several who sell mail-order, but there's nothing like paying them a visit to see what the plants look like 'in the flesh' if you can.

You will certainly need some 'oxygenating plants' which will add oxygen to the water, so helping to keep it clear. It's also a good idea to buy a water-lily or two. Not only do they look marvellous, but they shade the water, which is another factor in keeping it crystal clear.

All kinds of marginal plants are worthwhile, especially since, apart from providing form and flower for the pool edge, they also make a home for insects like the beautiful dragonflies.

Plant oxygenators either by fixing a weight to the clumps and throwing them in, or, better still, by pushing them into the mud at the bottom. A job for a sunny day!

Marginal plants are best planted in the soil but can be grown in their pots, provided they are covered with only a shallow depth of water.

Deep-water plants and water-lilies can be planted in the bottom of the pool if you can bear to get that wet and muddy. Alternatively, plant them in a special basket (obtainable from

When the planting has matured, an informal pool adds colour, interest and movement to the garden as well as attracting birds and insects.

all aquatic plant centres) in heavy soil and lower them in on a couple of strings held from either side of the pool. Some books suggest that they should be gradually lowered, setting them on bricks for a few days, lowering a little more, waiting a few days again, etc. This is in fact unnecessary. Just trim off the larger leaves and any dead or damaged growth and lower them straight to the bottom. But do make sure you don't 'drown' them by putting them deeper than they would naturally grow.

Bog plants, of course, are planted with a trowel in the normal way. But be sure you don't push the trowel through the liner!

Oxygenating plants

Pond-weed (Lagarosiphon major)
For a small pool, this is undoubtedly the one to go for. It will do the job without becoming over-vigorous and looks attractive under water.

For very shallow water or the mud at the water's edge

Marsh Marigold (Caltha palustris)
Bright glossy foliage topped by brilliant yellow buttercup flowers. The double form (*Caltha palustris* 'Plena') is even better, with more colourful flowers that last longer.

Lady's Smock (Cardamine pratensis 'Flore Pleno')
This is the double form of the well-known native, which I have recommended because it's not so rampant. It has small white or lilac flowers with yellow anthers in spring.

Golden Buttons(Cotula coronopifolia)
A small, spreading plant that is covered in yellow flowers all summer. Though short-lived it seeds itself freely.

Chameleon (Houttuynia cordata 'Chameleon')
A superb new foliage plant with leaves coloured green, cream and red. It runs freely but is easily controlled by simply pulling it out.

Monkey Musk (Mimulus luteus)
A very bright plant bearing a succession of small yellow flowers spotted red. Also recommended is the lavender musk (*Mimulus ringens*), with attractive blue flowers.

Marginal plants

Sweet Flag (Acorus calamus 'Variegatus')
A striking plant with brightly variegated, iris-like leaves. A bit vigorous for a small pool but easily controlled. Just lift it out and split it up.

Golden Club (Orontium aquaticum)
Well worth growing. The long, broad, waxy leaves glisten in the sunshine. The flowers are yellow and white and poker-like in May.

Bog Arum (Calla palustris)
This has glossy foliage and white flowers resembling the arum lily. It flowers in mid-summer and sometimes fruits too.

Iris (Iris laevigata)
One of the best of pool plants, this grows to about 18 inches (45 cm) tall and bears brilliant blue flowers in summer. There are several other forms with white or pink flowers and one with variegated foliage. If your pool is reasonably big, you'll have room for the yellow flag (*Iris pseudacorus*) and there is also a variegated variety of this species.

Pickerel Weed (Pontederia cordata)
Large clumps of handsome foliage with blue, delphinium-like flowers in late summer. Vigorous but easily divided.

Deep water plants

Water Hawthorn (Aponogeton distachyos)
The attractive leaves float on the surface. The flowers are white with a black centre and appear over a long period through spring and summer.

Water Violet (Hottonia palustris)
This could also be classified as an oxygenator because it does that job as well. It has deep lavender flowers held 6 inches (15 cm) above the water.

Water-lilies

Nymphaea pygmaea
A tiny lily suitable for water up to 6 inches (15 cm) deep, so

The large leaves of water-lilies help to shade the pool and therefore keep down green algae. They are available in a wide range of colours and for different sizes of pool.

perfect for the wooden-tub pool if it's rested on a brick. There are white, yellow and red varieties.

Nymphaea 'Froebeli'
One of the best for a small pool 9 inches to 2 feet (23–60 cm) deep. The flowers are blood-red.

Nymphaea laydekeri
Another type for water 9 inches to 2 feet (23–60 cm) deep. There are varieties with crimson, pink and purple flowers.

Nymphaea 'Escarboucle'
Perhaps the best of all water-lilies. The large, bright red flowers are very freely produced. Needs water 1 to 3 feet (30–90 cm) deep.

Nymphaea 'James Brydon'
Another popular variety for water 1 to 3 feet (30–90 cm) deep. It has huge, globe-shaped flowers of rose pink.

Nymphaea marliacea
Again for deeper water, there are varieties with white, yellow, red and pink flowers.

Pumps and electricity in the garden
Though it's by no means essential, it is not at all difficult to circulate the water by means of a small submersible pump. If it's a fountain you're after, you have no more to do than place

the pump in the pool at a level where the outlet will be above water, connect the electricity supply and turn on. Later you may feel you want to install a stream or a waterfall – but that's a subject for a book all on its own!

The one point I would make is this. Unless you are a very competent electrician, it's well worth getting a qualified electrical contractor to install the electricity supply. As you can imagine, the fact that pumps are actually placed in water makes them potentially dangerous.

Scree-gardens

Modern gardens are, on the whole, too small for a full-scale rock-garden. Nonetheless, alpine plants are amongst the most beautiful of all, so it would be a pity if they were excluded from the scheme of things. There are several ways they can be incorporated in the design.

1. To make a scree path, start by installing a wooden shuttering at the edges.
2. Set the slabs on well-drained compost and tap them down level.
3. Brush coarse grit between the slabs for added drainage and to enhance the effect.

4. Plant alpine plants through the gravel between the slabs. They will soon spread to soften the hard lines of the paving.

In the wild, most alpine plants live high up in the mountains, either wedged in crevices in rocks or growing in the gravel or 'scree' that collects at the bottoms of slopes. They therefore love cold, dry conditions and very good drainage. Indeed, it's quite difficult to get used to the idea that they will grow very happily in almost pure gravel with just a tiny amount of soil. What they hate is wet weather.

One way to grow them is in a stepping-stone path. This really is quite a good method for a small garden where paths, though necessary, are much begrudged because of the valuable space they occupy. This way they can be transformed into a floral feature that will delight you all the year round.

Of course, your scree-garden doesn't have to be in the form of a path. You can do the same thing by digging out a bed in the lawn perhaps, or, as I have done in my own garden, by making a circle of bricks with a path crossing the garden.

In a bed like that, you can also include some strategically placed rocks here and there. If you do, try to group them together to form natural-looking outcrops, rather than dotting them about. They never look quite natural that way.

Plants for the scree-garden

There are literally hundreds of alpine plants that will look good and do well in a scree-garden, so I will restrict myself to those that are easy to grow and rewarding. Once you start though, you'll find yourself wanting to collect more and more. There's no group of plants that is so notorious for getting the reluctant gardener hooked for life!

New Zealand Burr (Acaena)
These fairly vigorous carpeting plants will do well for a path but are perhaps too vigorous in the scree-bed. They form a carpet of small blue-grey leaves topped by bristly brown seed-heads.

Yarrow (Achillea)
There are several alpine yarrows, with aromatic, finely cut foliage and attractive yellow flowers. One of the best is *Achillea* 'King Edward', which bears sulphur-yellow flowers from May to September.

Rock Jasmine (Androsace)
Beautiful dwarf cushion or mat-forming alpines with white or pink flowers. They don't like wet, so could be a bit difficult. If possible, grow them in a cleft between two bits of rock where drainage will be better.

Antennaria dioica 'Rosea'
A very hardy carpeter, also ideal for paving. It has small, silvery leaves and small flowers varying from white to deep pink.

Columbine (Aquilegia)
Delightful little plants, but make sure you buy alpine species

or they'll be too big. I like *Aquilegia bertolonii*, with bright blue flowers. *A. discolor* is very tiny and has light blue flowers with creamy yellow cups. *A. scopulorum* is a bit bigger but has superb frilled foliage and flowers of light blue and primrose.

Sandwort (Arenaria grandiflora)
Bright green, mossy mats of foliage dotted with white flowers in late spring and early summer.

Thrift (Armeria)
A well-known, cushion-forming plant with globular pink flowers.

Aubrietia (Aubrieta deltoidea)
A well-known plant used widely in walls, where it makes a striking display. It can be used in paths and paving but tends to sprawl. Cut it back hard after flowering to keep the plants compact. There are many colours available and it's easy to raise from seed.

Bellflower (Campanula)
There are several species of bellflower which make good scree plants though some of them can become invasive. One of the best is *Campanula cochlearifolia* (sometimes called fairies' thimbles) which forms mats of fresh green foliage topped by tubby bells in many shades of blue or white.

Sea Heath (Frankenia)
Small, heather-like plants with clusters of tiny pink flowers at their tips.

Everlasting Flower (Helichrysum bellidioides)
A prostrate carpeter that can be a bit invasive but is easily cut back. It has white, woolly foliage and small white flowers.

Mint (Mentha requienii)
The last thing you might expect here is mint, but this one has minute leaves studded with lavender flowers in spring, and is very aromatic. It's ideal in a cool place.

White Cup (Nierembergia repens)
After mint, one of the potato family! A creeper with underground stems that forms mats of narrow, emerald-green leaves

covered in a profusion of small, cup-shaped white flowers in summer.

Pratia angulata
This is a mat-forming plant with fleshy, rounded leaves and delicate white, purple-streaked flowers.

Vegetable Sheep (Raoulia australis)
In fact, the name 'vegetable sheep' refers to another species of *Raoulia* but it's such a good name I couldn't resist attaching it to this one too. It refers to the fact that the tiny, silvery-white leaves make the plants look for all the world like sleeping sheep. This species is much smaller and forms mats of silvery-grey foliage covered in tiny yellow flowers in summer.

Pearlwort (Sagina glabra 'Aurea')
A creeping, moss-like plant with bright golden foliage.

Saxifrage (Saxifraga)
This is a great family and all are good in the scree-garden. They form carpets or low mounds, some with long spikes of flower, others studded with tiny stars of white, pink, red and yellow according to variety.

Stonecrop (Sedum)
A large group of plants with many species suitable for the scree-garden. One word of warning. I would avoid our native stonecrop, *Sedum acre*, which is sold widely in garden centres. It looks marvellous covered in bright yellow flowers, but it becomes a pernicious weed that you'll curse for years.

Houseleek (Sempervivum)
There are literally hundreds of species of these fascinating plants in cultivation, most of which are suitable for the scree-garden. They form mats of cactus-like rosettes which generally bear pink flowers.

Thyme (Thymus)
There several creeping thymes. Many will become invasive so a path is the best spot. The flowers range from white, through pink to deep red, and the small leaves are variegated in some varieties. My favourites are the lemon-scented *Thymus citrioides* and the very pale pink *Thymus serpyllum* 'Annie Hall'.

There are, of course, many dwarf bulbs that can be used in the scree-garden to very good effect. They can remain in the ground and will poke their heads through carpeting alpines in the spring to give a welcome show of flower.

Pergolas

When they ran out of space in New York, what did they do? They went upwards. And that's exactly what we should be doing in our small gardens too. We should take every opportunity to put up structures that will carry plants skywards to give the garden a truly three-dimensional effect.

Where there's an entrance into the garden, it can be beautified with an arch over which roses and other climbers could be trained. Better still, develop the archway to form a covered walk, by building a pergola. As you can imagine, a pergola built, for example, over the scree-garden path would be a riot of colour not only the length of the path but up to 8 feet (244 cm) above it too!

Kits are available at garden centres and these are undoubtedly the best bet. They are not expensive but, if the budget is tight, you could reduce the cost by buying second-hand timber from the demolition contractor and making your own.

The kits are extremely easy to erect. Here I would certainly use the metal sockets that are just driven into the soil. Unlike with fencing panels, there is little or no wind resistance to worry about.

It's important to keep the pergola level, so the amount you drive in the metal spikes is critical. There are two alternatives.

Drive in the first spike and fix the post in it. Then measure

Pergolas are available in kit form and are easy to erect with just a hammer and screwdriver.

the required distance for the next spike, using one of the pergola rails. Bang in the spike and put the post loosely in the socket. Then put a straight-edge on top of the posts and check for level with a spirit-level.

Because the posts are 8 feet (244 cm) high, that's not so easy, so you may prefer either to remove the first post and check the level of the tops of the sockets, or to measure 3 feet (90 cm) up each post, bang a nail halfway in and rest the straight-edge on that.

The side-rails can then be nailed on using galvanised nails, and the cross-bars are pre-jointed so they simply slot over the top. Just like the fencing, make sure that you put the pergola up section by section as you go along. Putting all the posts in and hoping the cross-struts will fit is chancing your luck just a bit too much!

What you do with the posts now depends a bit on what you want to grow up the pergola. If it's to be roses, for example, you can train them up simply by tying them to the posts with string. But clematis needs different treatment. They climb by twisting their leaf stalks round anything they can find. They'll happily climb up a wire, but the pergola post is, of course, too thick.

The best bet is to fix a wire tightly top and bottom of the post, one on each side. Then force a piece of 1-inch (2.5 cm) thick wood under the wire to hold it away from the post so that the plant has room to get round it. Nail the piece of wood in place to stop it moving.

However, there's nothing to stop you having the best of both worlds and using the rose as an anchorage for the clematis so that you get the benefit of two sessions of flower. Other, more vigorous, twiners like honeysuckle would need to be grown on their own and the wire technique is ideal for them too.

For a list of climbers suitable for pergolas and fences see page 152.

Raised beds

Acid-loving plants (often referred to as 'ericaceous' plants) are amongst the most beautiful of them all. The rhododendrons and azaleas make a flamboyant show in spring and early summer, while heathers will carpet the ground with flower. The beautiful pieris with its brilliant red young growths in spring and the delicate divided foliage of the Japanese maples are not to be missed. And miss them you

There's no need to feel deprived if your soil is limey. By building a raised bed, you can still grow the acid-lovers. This bed was made with old railway sleepers.

driving in posts around the perimeter. The posts should be of pressure-treated timber and fairly stout. As you drive them in, level the tops roughly so that they come to a height slightly less than that of the log-roll. Then just roll out the log-roll and either nail or wire it to the posts so that the posts are on the inside and will be hidden when the enclosure is filled.

My own choice would be railway sleepers. These are fairly readily available – have a look in the classified ads in a farming magazine – and not as expensive as you may imagine. The only problem is cutting them and if you have a lot to do, it's worth hiring a chain-saw. Otherwise, an ordinary bow-saw with a new blade and a lot of elbow-grease will suffice.

They are fixed in much the same way as the log-rolls. Drive in some posts around the perimeter of the bed, lay out the sleepers and fix them to the posts. Generally two sleepers will be high enough. Of course, it's not feasible to nail the sleeper to the post because it's too thick, so either nail the post to the sleeper or bang a couple of large staples into the sleeper, one either side of the post, and fix it with wire.

Another good alternative is to make the walls with peat-blocks. These look very attractive indeed in an informal setting and they last much longer than you might think. Certainly, once they are held together by plant roots, they'll be there for 15 years or more.

You can buy peat blocks at most garden centres. The most important thing is that they must be really wet – not just moist – when you use them. So each one must be soaked in a tank of water for a while before use.

Start by marking out the area and levelling the soil. Then put down a 2-inch (5 cm) layer of sphagnum peat to bed in the first layer of blocks. When they are put down they should be sloped very slightly backwards into the bed. When the first row is completed, fill in behind with peat and press some more in the cracks between the blocks.

The second row should be 'bonded' just like a brick wall. It should also finish slightly set back from the first and, again, sloping backwards. Once more, when that row is in place, fill in behind with peat to bring it up to the top of the blocks and then set the next row in the same way. Again, this one should be bonded and should slope backwards slightly.

If you like, you can plant between the blocks as you go, though quite honestly it isn't difficult to force the root-balls of small plants into the cracks in the wall afterwards. It's not a good idea to go more than about four blocks high and shouldn't be necessary anyway.

When you fill the bed you'll need to find some acid soil from somewhere. Your local garden centre should be able to advise you of a source, though it may be an idea to do a simple lime-test before you buy it. Use the soil to make up a special compost using 5 parts soil to 2 parts peat and 1 part course grit.

If you can't find acid soil anywhere, you'll have to make do with peat and sharp, lime-free sand mixed about 50:50. Bear in mind, though, that this contains no nutrients at all so you'll need to add fertiliser. Mix about a $3\frac{1}{2}$-inch (9 cm) flower-potful of blood, fish and bone fertiliser with a barrow-load of compost. Later on, you'll need to feed at least twice a year, in February and again in June, using about two handfuls per square yard (sq. m) of bed. This annual feeding should be done for a soil-filled bed also.

Acid-loving plants

Japanese Maple (Acer palmatum)
Though these beautiful shrubs and small trees will survive on soils with some lime, they are much happier in a moist, acid soil, out of the wind. There are several varieties available, the majority making a large shrub or small tree. The variety 'Atropurpureum' has striking bronze-purple leaves while 'Aureum' is golden yellow. Quite different is the irresistible 'Dissectum'. This forms a small, gnarled tree of exquisite shape. The leaves are finely divided to make a wonderful lacy canopy. Perhaps the most popular variety is 'Dissectum Atropurpureum' which has deep red leaves, but my own favourite is 'Dissectum Flavescens' which has fresh, soft, yellow-green foliage. Look out also for the variety 'Senkaki', the 'coral-bark maple', which has beautifully-shaped green leaves turning canary-yellow in autumn, and bright coral-red bark in winter.

Camellia
Showy, medium-sized shrubs with glossy evergreen foliage and exotic-looking, rose-shaped flowers in spring. There are many colours available according to variety, from pure white through pink to deep red. Ideally, plant them in a position where they won't get full sunlight first thing in the morning as this tends to scorch blooms, especially if they're frozen.

Winter Hazel (Corylopsis pauciflora)
A spreading shrub up to about 6 feet (180 cm) high with delightful, pendulous yellow flowers in early spring. The young leaves are tinged pink.

Heather (Erica)
Though the winter-flowering heathers are generally lime-tolerant, those that flower in the summer are not. There is a range of flower colour according to species and variety and many superb foliage varieties too.

Checkerberry (Gaultheria procumbens)
A creeping evergreen, forming carpets of dark green leaves and bearing bright red berries in autumn and winter.

Sweetspire (Itea ilicifolia)
A medium-sized, holly-like evergreen shrub with long, droop-

ing, catkin-like flowers of fragrant greenish-white in late summer.

Gentian (*Gentiana septemfida, Gentiana sino-ornata*)

The gentians are superlative herbaceous perennials with the most striking blue coloration of any flower. Many are difficult to grow but nothing could be easier than these two. *Gentiana septemfida* flowers in July and August while *G. sino-ornata* follows from September to November.

Calico Bush (*Kalmia latifolia*)

A marvellous medium-sized shrub very similar to rhododendron. Clusters of bright pink, saucer-shaped flowers in June.

Lithospermum diffusum 'Heavenly Blue'

A carpeting evergreen shrub, covered in gentian-blue flowers all summer.

Magnolia

Magnificent, generally large shrubs. Most are much too large for the small garden and you should not be seduced into buying the beautiful *Magnolia soulangeana*, for example, unless you have a very big garden. But your raised bed could accommodate *M. stellata* which is much smaller and slow-growing. The white, fragrant, star-shaped flowers are profusely borne in March and April. Look out, too, for the forms 'Rosea' and 'Rubra' which are pink-flushed.

Pernettya (*Pernettya mucronata*)

Certainly the showiest of all the dwarf evergreens when in fruit. The plants are covered with hundreds of white flowers in June, followed by large, shiny berries ranging in colour from glistening white through pink to deep purple. In order to ensure berrying, it's best to plant in groups of three or four with at least one male form. If the garden centre can't provide you with a guaranteed male, go elsewhere where they can.

Pieris

Highly ornamental evergreen shrubs and a real 'must' for the small garden because they really work for their living. The foliage is shiny and attractive in its own right, while the flowers which form in the autumn brighten up the winter as red buds. In April or May they open to form tassels of white flowers rather like lily-of-the-valley. And, as if that were not enough, the young shoots are coloured flaming red or in some cases pink, changing with age through pink and creamy white to green. Recommended varieties are: *Pieris* 'Forest Flame', *P. formosa* 'Wakehurst' and the variegated form, *P. japonica* 'Variegata' which has green and cream leaves flushed pink when young.

Rhododendron

Deservedly popular evergreen shrubs with perhaps the most luxuriant flowers of all our cultivated shrubs. There are hundreds of varieties to choose from, but many of them are far too big for the small garden. Look for the dwarf varieties like 'Bluebird', 'Pink Drift' or 'Scarlet Wonder', or go for the new hybrids of *Rhododendron yakushimanum*. These are rounded, compact bushes growing no more than about 3 to 4 feet (90–122 cm) high and covered in exotic flowers of many colours according to variety. Rhododendrons prefer a slightly shaded position.

Azalea

These are also of the rhododendron family and require the same conditions. Unlike rhododendrons though, there are varieties that lose their leaves in winter as well as the evergreens. Nonetheless, the deciduous azaleas are not to be despised, because they will give a real technicolor show over a long period. The trumpet-shaped flowers come in the spring in various colours according to variety. Then, in autumn, the leaves turn fiery red, orange and yellow. Well worth a place in the bed. The evergreen, or Japanese, azaleas will grow to 3 to 4 feet (90–120 cm) and slowly form spreading bushes. Again, they are available in all the colours of the rainbow.

PLANTING

Plants, of course, are what gardens and gardening are all about. Though the Japanese seem to get by with a few rocks and a patch of sand, I simply can't imagine such a thing as a garden without plants. What's more, however 'green' you may be now, I can guarantee that it will only take one season of gardening for you to become as enthusiastic about growing them as I am. But I have to admit that, to the newcomer, it can be a minefield!

You'll find lots of useful advice about planting the herbaceous border with monocotyledons or about the value of epiphytes in the pinetum, which is great when you don't know the difference between a bulb and a biennial! And, if you're building your first garden, there's not the slightest reason why you should.

So, if the old hands would just nod off to sleep for a few minutes, I'll explain!

Types of plants

If you look for them, of course you can find all kinds of complications in the field of garden plants. There are quite a few differences, for example, between botanical and horticultural definitions and many grey areas, over which august gentlemen with microscopes and Latin dictionaries have been arguing for generations. Well, you can forget all that for a start!

Gardeners, as opposed to plant collectors, have simplifed the language considerably so it's not nearly as difficult as it looks at first sight. Here's my simple glossary—

Tree

Of course everyone knows what a tree is, but there are two distinct types sold in garden centres these days. A 'standard' or 'half-standard' tree has a clean stem up to about 6 feet (180 cm) or 4 ft (120 cm) respectively, with a 'crown' of branches on the top. That's the traditional way of buying trees.

But these days, many trees are sold 'feathered'. That means that, though they still have a central stem, the side-branches have been left on to give the appearance of a large bush. With this type of tree, you can either grow it as it comes, leaving the side-branches on, or you can, at a later stage, prune it into a standard tree (see page 134).

1. A traditional standard or half-standard tree has a clean stem with a 'crown' of branches at the top.
2. A 'feathered' tree has been allowed to retain its side-branches. It can be grown like this or the bottom branches can be pruned back hard to make a traditional standard.

Most trees are deciduous, which means they lose their leaves in winter, while a few are evergreen, retaining their leaves.

Shrub

This is a woody plant that is grown as a bush rather than on a clean stem like a tree. All will grow in the garden for many years without dying down in the winter. Some shrubs are deciduous, losing their leaves in winter, while there are many more evergreen shrubs than trees. Typical shrubs you might find in the garden centre are flowering currant, forsythia and rhododendron.

Conifer

A plant that bears cones, but generally an evergreen with many small, hard, stem-like leaves. Conifers are typified by the tall, narrow hedging shrubs like the Lawson's cypress though not all are upright-growing. There are several useful conifers which will hug the ground too.

Rose

Again, we all know that roses are those prickly shrubs with the beautiful flowers that have for ever been the joy of young women and a source of acute embarrassment to young men! There are many different types, which can again be conveniently classified.

Hybrid teas – medium-sized bushes with a long flowering period and generally one, perfectly-shaped bloom per stem.
Floribundas – again medium-sized, long-flowering bushes

with clusters of flowers on the same stem. *Miniatures* – small plants like tiny floribundas. *Climbers* – just like floribundas or hybrid teas in flower but with a climbing habit. *Ramblers* – a climbing or sprawling habit and normally with just one or sometimes two flushes of flower. *Shrub roses* – these are very variable but generally make much bigger bushes with a shorter flowering period.

Climbers

As the name implies, these plants have a vigorous habit of growth and are used to cover fences or walls or to grow through trees and other shrubs. Most are perennial and shrubby, though there are a few herbaceous perennials and annuals. Examples of climbers are clematis, wisteria and honeysuckle.

Alpines

Plants from higher regions generally grown in the rock-garden. Examples are houseleeks and stonecrops.

Perennials

The word actually refers to plants that will live for many years, some dying down in winter but reappearing in spring. But in gardening terms it generally applies to herbaceous perennials. These are soft-stemmed plants, most of which die down in winter but come up again even bigger in spring. Unfortunately, they have a variety of other names too and which one is used depends upon the whim of the nursery or garden centre. They are known as perennials, hardy perennials, herbaceous perennials, hardy plants, border plants or hardy border plants. Examples are lupins, delphiniums and carnations. To complicate matters slightly, there are a few tender perennials grown too. These are plants that will live for a long time but need protection from frost, like geraniums.

Biennials

Plants that are planted one year, flower the next and are then pulled out. Examples are wallflowers and sweet williams. Botanically, some biennials are actually perennial but, since they flower best in the first year, they're grown as biennials, and all gardeners know them as biennials, so don't worry about it.

Annuals

Plants that flower in the same year that they're sown and then

Above. A floribunda rose carries its blooms in clusters of smaller flowers. This is the very popular Iceberg. *Opposite.* Hybrid tea roses have one bloom per stem. They are generally better shaped than floribundas. This is the popular Sunblest.

die. There are hardy annuals which will stand mild frosts so can be sown directly outside, and half-hardies which need starting inside and should not be planted out until all danger of frost has passed. They are sold in garden centres as 'bedding plants'.

Bulbs
Botanically, there are bulbs, corms, rhizomes and tubers, but I would lump them all together. They are all plants with fleshy storage organs below ground, and are often bought in a dry state. Remember that the bulk of spring and autumn-flowering bulbs are hardy so can be left in the ground for

ever, where they'll multiply like mad, while most summer-flowerers are tender and have to be lifted each autumn. Hardies include daffodils, crocus and snowdrops, while the tender ones are things like dahlias and gladioli.

Patio plants

Some garden centres now sell what they call 'patio plants'. These are big, attractive plants in decorative pots. They're ideal for brightening up the patio, but bear in mind that some are not entirely hardy. Enquire and only buy the tender types if you can protect them from frost in winter.

Ericaceous plants

I include this category purely because it's a word still used sometimes by nurseries trying to blind you with science! It simply means 'acid-loving', so unless you *know* you have acid soil or can provide it, don't buy them.

Planning the borders

What a headache! Here you are with the choice of literally thousands of plants, few of which you really know, and you somehow have to plant them in the right place. First of all you have to think about aspect – whether this particular plant likes sun or shade, wet or dry, acid or limy soil. They need to be positioned so that when they grow they exactly fill their allotted space, provide a show of colour all year round without one colour clashing with the other and they have to be planted according to their correct height and spread so that one doesn't hide or smother its neighbour. The number of different permutations is endless.

Put like that, it's enough to put you off for life, but fortunately it's not nearly as difficult as it sounds. Nonetheless, it's still worth finding out as much about plants as possible.

I have already suggested that you get yourself a few good, comprehensive nursery catalogues and a plant reference book or two. Also that you should get around to visit gardens open to the public, nurseries, botanic gardens and garden centres, just to see as many plants as possible. The more you know about your plants, the more fun your garden will become.

But above all, take your time. I wouldn't expect to plant the whole garden in the first year or even the second, come to that. It's much better to buy slowly as you find plants you really can't live without (as you surely will) than to fill the whole garden in one go. While you're waiting, you can fill the borders with hardy annuals, which are the cheapest and most cheerful experience you'll ever treat yourself to, or with half-hardy bedding.

But when it comes to planning, how can you translate those magnificent herbaceous borders, shrubberies and rose gardens of the stately-home gardens to your own little semi-detached plot? Well, you don't have to.

All that grandiose stuff went out with debutantes. No one has the space or the money for it any more so we need to look for a different style of gardening. And the answer, in my opinion, lies in the old cottage gardens of our great grand-fathers – well almost anyway.

They had much the same problem of lack of space as we do and their answer was to bung everything in the same border in what looked like a higgledy-piggledy fashion. Lupins and hollyhocks jostled with herbs for the medicine chest, while marigolds and roses fought for space with lettuces and beetroot. Every inch of soil was used and it looked marvellous! We can use exactly the same technique in the gardens of modern houses. You don't have to have a thatched roof and a rustic porch to plant yourself a cottage garden! What's more, we have a much more exciting range of plants to choose from, including many improved varieties of those self-same plants our great-grandfathers grew. So the modern cottage garden can look even better than a chocolate-box.

Now I'm not suggesting that this kind of scheme is easy to perfect, especially if you are not well acquainted with the plants. But you'll be pleased to hear that there is a perfect let-out.

You see, there's a whole range of plants that can be lifted and replanted *even when they're in full flower*. Nearly all the herbaceous perennials are so accommodating that they'll wilt for no more than a day or two and then recover to their previous glory. So, all you have to do is to plant your border as well as you can and then, if you find you've made a mistake, simply pour a bucket of water over the plant in the wrong position, lift it with as much root as possible and transplant it where it looks right. Then give it another bucket of water and it'll never look back!

However, I wouldn't like to recommend the same treatment for trees and shrubs. Mind you, if you find they're in the wrong place you can, with a bit of upheaval, lift and replant in the dormant season during autumn or early spring, but generally they like to get their roots down and establish themselves.

Still, when you think about it, that makes the job a lot easier. Herbaceous plants, alpines and bulbs can all be lifted in flower, and annuals and biennials will only be there for one season anyway, so all you really have to get right first time are the trees and shrubs. And if you make a mistake there, you can still rectify it at the small cost of slowing the plants' growth down a bit. I hope that sets your mind at rest a little!

Buying plants

Most garden centres and nurseries are a pretty respectable bunch and the trade in general is averse to ripping off its customers. What's more, most are aware of the need for good quality control and would rather throw away a bad plant than sell it. So all in all, you can expect a fair deal, even though you may be a bit in the dark about what you're buying. But they are all in the business of making a profit, so they are sometimes not quite as saintly as they would have you believe!

I have never, for example, seen a notice in a garden centre warning customers not to buy the expensive rhododendrons until they have tested their soil for lime. I have often seen garden centres selling frost-tender bedding plants in May when there is every likelihood of a cold snap. And, though most have made a big effort in the past 10 years to upgrade quality, there are still a few who are happy to sell you rubbish. Inevitable I suppose.

My first rule when buying plants is perhaps the most difficult to adhere to. Never buy on impulse.

It's a well-known fact in the business that you can sell anything that's in flower. It's obvious, really, that plants become very difficult to resist when they are looking blooming beautiful. But resist them you must.

When you go plant shopping, take a good plant book or a comprehensive nurseryman's catalogue with you. Then you'll be able to look up that irresistible buy to see whether or not it will suit your soil, position and space. If it's not listed in your book, ask before you buy and, if they can't, or won't, tell you all the details, leave it where it is.

Assessing good quality is sometimes difficult. Often, the best plants are the smaller, less dramatic-looking ones and they are often the cheapest too!

It would be fair to say that buying herbaceous perennials is not really a problem. Almost anything you buy, so long as it's actually alive, will grow and flourish in most gardens in a fairly short time. But buying trees and shrubs takes more care.

First of all, look at the pot. If it's full of weeds, my advice would be to get in your car and go elsewhere. Obvious neglect almost certainly means that other important cultural practices have also been neglected, so the plants are likely not to have been fed and watered correctly, pruned or repotted. Have a special look at the bottom of the pot. If a mass of roots is showing through, the plant will be pot-bound and will take a long time to establish after planting and start into regrowth. That kind of garden centre doesn't deserve your business.

If you're buying in the spring or early summer, just lift the plant by its top-growth to make sure it's well rooted in the pot. If it looks as though you're going to pull it out of the compost, it has just been repotted and will suffer on transplanting.

When you've found the plants you want, sort through them to find the best of the bunch. This is not necessarily the tallest – in fact often the reverse is the case. I would always buy the *bushiest* plant in the row, making sure it's compact and well shaped and has no damage to the branches.

If you're buying climbers, reject those with a long length of bare stem and all the growth at the top. Look for the one with a number of shoots right at the bottom. Even if the top part of the plant looks dead, this is still the best one to go for. Conifers must never show any sign of brown foliage. This is often due to wind damage or to the pots freezing in winter and, with most conifers, it will not grow out.

Trees should be well shaped and have a good, well-balanced head if they are standards or half-standards. They should also be standing upright. Yes, I know that sounds pernickety but, if they have been growing on the slant, they haven't been fed and watered properly because the pot has not been level.

Sometimes, it may be better to buy trees and shrubs from a nursery rather than a garden centre. Most garden-centre plants are container-grown and are therefore generally restricted in size and more expensive. On the other hand, trees or shrubs grown in the field and lifted bare-rooted are in most cases bigger and cheaper. However, they can only be lifted and planted in the dormant season between November and the end of March. But, if you have the patience and are lucky enough to have a good, old-fashioned nursery within reasonable distance, you will almost always get a better bargain. Indeed, if you buy a hedge of one of the cheaper plants like quickthorn or privet, this may well be the *only* way to buy them.

In my view, fruit trees should also be bought from a specialist grower if possible. While many garden centres do sell a reasonable range of trees, a specialist will have a wider choice of varieties which will also be generally cheaper, and he'll be able to guarantee them free from disease. It's also much wiser to buy one-year-old or, at most, two-year-old trees. One-year-old apples and pears, for example, while costing less, will start to fruit much earlier than older trees you are likely to be offered in the garden centre.

Buying bulbs is generally easy since the quality overall is pretty good. However, it's as well to press each bulb and to reject any that feel spongy. Naturally, if you see any sign of disease or damage, leave them on the shelf.

A few bulbs really shouldn't be sold at all in the dry state. Two notable examples are hardy cyclamen and snowdrops. They are generally much too dry ever to grow and, once planted, that's the last you're likely to see of them! These are much better bought either from a nursery, which can guarantee to lift them and send them straight out, or in pots where you *know* they're growing.

Buying plants through mail-order is often fraught with problems and that's a pity because it's often a way to get hold of less usual varieties that garden centres don't stock. I certainly wouldn't advise against mail-order, provided you stick to a couple of basic rules.

First of all, never expect a bargain. The newspaper advertisements you will see offering plants at 30 for a penny ha'-penny are best used for wrapping the fish and chips. They will be tiny rooted cuttings and very difficult to get established.

Secondly, avoid ads that go into great eulogies about this wonderful new plant but don't tell you the proper Latin name of it. Instead they invent a fancy name of their own so you'll never really know what you're buying. The wonderful rose hedges are a perfect example. The artist's impression of a perfectly clipped hedge smothered in masses of marvellous blooms the size of a cabbage is misleading in the extreme. What you generally get is something very like the common wild rose that sprawls all over the garden and has a couple of fairly nondescript pink flowers for a few weeks every year – and of course absolutely nothing in winter.

Remember, too, that your rights are well protected. If you are not satisfied with the plants you receive, you should send them back immediately and demand they give you a refund.

But most mail-order nurseries are highly respectable places and are anxious to provide good quality and service. Naturally even they make mistakes from time to time though, so, if you're not satisfied, again at least give them a chance to put things right. Most will.

Finally, when you do find a mail-order nursery that sends you good-quality plants, well wrapped and at a fair price – stick with them.

Plants in pre-packs bought from department stores or supermarkets are another tricky proposition. Cheap they certainly are and some are quite good. But a store is the worst place in the world to keep plants, which deteriorate rapidly. So unless you can see the plant clearly through the plastic and it is obviously healthy and unshrivelled, it's best to leave it alone.

Just a word about bedding plants, though I have already hinted at the dangers. In most parts of the country, it's unwise to plant them outside until the first week in June, when all danger of frost should be past. Further north, it could be even later. This goes for all half-hardies, whether they be the boxed annuals or the perennials in pots, like geraniums and fuchsias.

Again, because of the rule that anything in flower will sell quickly, most summer bedding will be in flower when you buy it. Remember that in some cases this could mean that they'll finish earlier too, so it's sometimes a good idea to buy those that haven't started to flower yet.

Important planting rules

I'm afraid I tend to get a bit worked up on the subject of planting. The reason is that so many new gardeners spend a lot of money on plants and then, through carelessness, or more often through ignorance of the correct technique, allow them to die. It's a sorry fact, but a true one, that over half the trees and shrubs planted each year die in the first season. So bear with me if I chunter on and take care you follow the instructions to the letter!

First the general rules that apply to all plants.

Always plant at the right time of year. Most deciduous trees and shrubs (those that lose their leaves) will actually do better if they're planted in the autumn – from the end of October to about mid-December. The reason for this is that the soil is then warm from a summer of sunshine and it's unlikely at that time to dry out. What's more, as soon as leaves fall from deciduous plants they naturally put on a spurt of root growth. So they'll start growing immediately and get established before the real cold sets in. Then they'll be ready for a flying start in spring.

Of course, if deciduous trees and shrubs are bare-rooted instead of container-grown, they *must* be planted in the dormant season between the end of October and March.

Evergreen trees and shrubs are better planted either in September or in April or May. But if you do leave them until the spring, it's *vital* that you water them regularly if the weather turns dry.

Most herbaceous perennials can also be planted in the early autumn. But if you're in the least worried about their hardiness, leave it until the spring. I'm convinced that plants that are on the borderline of hardiness will stand a much better chance of survival if they are allowed to get established in the milder weather and then get the shock of a cold winter rather more slowly.

There are generally two planting times for bulbs, in the autumn for the spring-flowerers like daffs and crocus and in the spring for the summer-flowering types like lilies and gladioli. As I've already pointed out, there are some, like snowdrops and hardy cyclamen, that are best planted immediately after flowering, or from pots.

Most biennials can go in during the early autumn but always leave half-hardy bedding plants until the last frost is well and truly behind you. They're expensive and just not worth the risk of earlier planting.

In a new garden, soil improvement will generally be necessary for all plants. But it's folly just to dig a hole in uncultivated soil and add organic matter to the material you have dug out. However much you improve a small planting area, it will always be subject to problems, more especially on heavy soils.

If you dig a hole in otherwise uncultivated land, it tends to act like a sump, draining water from the soil around it and surrounding the roots with wet, cold earth. At best it will slow growth; at worst it will actually drown the roots and kill the tree.

So leave your planting until you've had the chance to cultivate the whole border (see pages 38–43).

But, even with the border cultivated, you may still have to add extra organic matter. If the land is heavy, it's likely to come out in large lumps which will be difficult or impossible to break down to a fine soil. Bear in mind that the roots need to be completely surrounded by soil with as few large air pockets as possible. If it's not fine enough to allow that, mix some moist peat with it. Incidentally, it really is important to ensure that the peat *is* moist. If you use it dry, it's very hard to wet again and could actually do more harm than good.

Planting instructions always include the advice, 'add a handful of bonemeal'. I can't for the life of me think why. Certainly it's the stuff to use in winter when only the roots may be active, but at any other time of year the plant will need the full range of plant nutrients. So enrich the soil with either rose fertiliser or Growmore.

After planting, the *most* vital part of the whole operation is to water as and when it becomes necessary. With bare-rooted plants, in autumn it may not have to be done at all because the weather is likely to be wet anyway. But at any other time, and especially with pot-grown plants, it's *the difference between life and death*. Well, I warned you I was likely to get melodramatic, but it grieves me that the already high failure rate after planting rose in the drought year of 1976 to a staggering 90 per cent! That, for me, is enough evidence to show that most failures are due to nothing more than lack of water.

Watering doesn't mean a little sprinkle from the watering-can either. The soil around the plant must be *saturated*. If you just add a little, the roots tend to come to the surface in search of water and there, of course, they are even more at risk from hot sunshine. So put the hose on the roots until the soil is soaked right down to the lower levels, especially if you're planting in the summer.

Planting trees and shrubs

The technique varies a little depending on whether the plants are bought bare-rooted or in containers. As I've already said, plants in containers can be planted at any time of the year while bare-rooted trees and shrubs must go in at the right time.

The first rule when planting bare-rooted plants is to keep the roots covered either with soil or with a wet sack, at all times. The tiny roots that take up water and nutrients will die if they are exposed to drying winds or if they're left in the sun, so make sure they stay moist.

If plants arrive at a time when it's impossible to plant them immediately, they must have their roots covered. The best way is to 'heel' them in. To do this, you simply dig a trench,

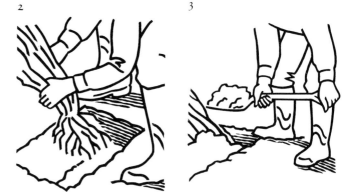

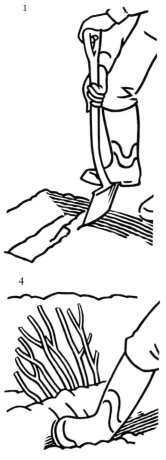

1. If bare-rooted plants cannot be planted straight away they should be heeled in. Dig a trench throwing the soil forward.
2. Put the roots of the plants in the trench, leaning them slightly against the soil you have dug out.
3. Dig another trench behind the plants, again throwing the soil forward to cover the roots.
4. Put your boot on the soil to firm it round the roots. In winter, plants can stay like this for some time.

throwing the soil forwards as you do. Lay the plants in the trench with the roots in the bottom and the tops leaning at an angle, resting on the soil at the back. Then cover the roots by digging another trench and throwing the soil forwards. Leaning them at a slight angle simply prevents strong winds loosening them in the soil.

Plants should not be planted in winter when the soil is frozen and this can also make it difficult to heel them in. In this case they are best left in their wrappings in a frost-free shed or garage until the weather gets a bit better.

If plants arrive with roots looking a bit dry, soak them in a bucket of water for an hour or two before planting.

You will already have prepared the border by deep-digging, working in organic matter (see pages 41–42).

Dig a hole large enough to take the roots of the plant when fully spread out. While you're checking that it's big enough, also have a look at the roots and remove any that are broken, cutting them back cleanly with a sharp knife or secateurs. If there are broken shoots, these can also be cut back to a point just above a bud at the same time.

Trees will need to be staked and this is best done before planting to avoid damaging the roots. Recent research has shown that it's best to support the tree with only a short stake, certainly no more than a third the length of the stem. This will allow the top of the tree to sway about in the wind, which has the effect of strengthening the base of the stem and the root system. Happily, it's also cheaper!

Hammer the stake in well and then set the plant up against

it, making sure that the tree will finish at exactly the same level it was when it was growing on the nursery. This is really *very* important since some trees will simply give up the ghost if they go in too deeply. You'll be able to tell the correct depth by a clear soil mark on the stem.

If the soil you have dug out is still heavy and lumpy, now's the time to add peat to the pile as previously suggested. Put on a couple of handfuls of fertiliser, too, and then knock a little soil onto the roots.

Grab the stem of the tree and jerk it up and down a little to work some of the soil between the roots, and then push a bit more soil into the hole. When it's half full, tread it down firmly but gently. If the soil is dry you can be a bit more heavy-footed, but if it's wet, use the sole of your boot and be gentle. Then refill completely and firm again.

Fix the tree to the stake with a proper plastic tree tie. I know this adds to the expense but it really does help to ensure survival. Whatever you do, *never* use either wire or nylon string. Both will cut into the bark and eventually certainly kill the tree.

Finally, fix the plastic tie with a little nail in the stake and tidy up around it by scratching out your footmarks with a fork. If you have any handy, a good mulch of manure, peat or shredded bark will help prevent weed growth and conserve moisture.

Bare-rooted shrubs are planted in exactly the same way except, of course, that no stake is needed.

Container-grown trees are a bit different. First of all, if you buy the plants in the winter and discover that you can't plant them immediately for one reason or another, the roots should, like the bare-rooted trees, be protected. But this time you need to protect them from freezing. You can do this either by digging the pot into the soil or by heaping peat, bark or any other loose material around them. This is especially important with evergreens which can suffer quite badly in cold winters. Being green all the time, they are continually losing water and, if the roots are allowed to freeze, they find it impossible to replace what they've lost. On sunny winter days, that could lead to browning of the leaves.

At any time of the year, bear in mind that they will need watering. If you buy plants in summer and can't get them in straight away, you must water the pots daily.

Watering is most important before planting too. Never, never plant anything that has dry roots because you'll find

1. When planting container-grown trees, prepare the soil first and dig a hole twice the size of the root-ball.
2. Place the tree, still in its pot, in the hole to check that the top of the root-ball is at the correct level.

3. Water the pot well before planting, even if it seems wet already, and remove the pot by carefully cutting it off.
4. If your soil is heavy, improve it by adding peat to the soil you have dug out.

5. If you are planting in the growing season, put a couple of handfuls of general fertiliser on the pile. In winter use bone-meal.
6. Put the pot in the hole and refill halfway, using the best of the topsoil you have dug out.

Continued from page 132.
7. Firm the soil around the plant with your boot. If the soil is on the wet side, don't overdo it.
8. Hammer in a stake that is long enough to reach a third of the way up the stem. Don't put it through the root-ball.
9. Secure the tree with a proper plastic tie, using a collar to prevent rubbing on the stake.

Shrubs are planted in exactly the same way as trees except that there is no need to use a stake.

them very difficult to wet again once they're in the soil.

Remove the pot and then plant the tree in the way recommended for bare-rooted plants but with a couple of slight differences. First of all, the width of the root-ball will prevent you setting the tree close to the stake. So you must either use two stakes, one either side of the hole with a cross-bar nailed to them, or slope the stake a little.

This time, there's no need to look for a soil mark on the stem to ensure that the tree is planted at the right level. Simply put a cane across the hole and ensure that the top of the container comes level with it. A little more care is needed when firming soil around the ball. Never tread directly on top of the root-ball, but firm around it.

Again, shrubs are planted in just the same way but without the stake.

Now for the most important part of the whole operation. If you plant at any time other than the winter, it's absolutely vital to water the plants in immediately after planting. And then you must keep an eye on them and water them again whenever necessary.

It's a good idea to make a wall of soil around the plants so that you can put the hose inside and leave it running for a while to really soak the soil. Certainly it's not a lot of good watering with a small watering-can unless you're happy to run backwards and forwards to the tap many times. But do *please* (I can't say it often enough) avoid throwing your money down the drain by forgetting this most important of tasks. There, I think I've made my point!

Standard and half-standard trees need no pruning after planting as a rule. But, if you've bought a 'feathered' tree, which is quite likely if you buy from a garden centre, and you want to turn it into a standard or half-standard with a length of bare stem, you'll have to prune off the side-branches up to the point at which you want the 'crown' of branches to start. I would advise leaving this job until the autumn because those extra side-shoots will help to fatten up the main stem. Then cut them right back to the main stem with a pair of sharp secateurs and pare the stub back with a sharp knife to make a really smooth, neat-looking finish.

Planting climbers
Climbers can be divided into three groups depending on their habit of growth. First of all there are the self-clingers. Plants like Virginia creeper, ivy and the climbing hydrangea need no

support at all and will cling to the house wall or the fence. They will, incidentally, do no damage to the walls of modern houses where the mortar is strong. On old houses they'll anchor themselves where there is crumbling mortar but even there they will only do damage if they are pulled off the wall.

The clingers and the twiners will both need support. These include plants like clematis which holds on by twining its leaf stalks around a support, or honeysuckle which twists its stems around things. They will need to be supported on wires or trellis.

The easiest way is to fix wires to the fence posts with staples. You can strain the wire tight by wrapping it round a short length of wood which is used like a lever. Start about 2 feet (60 cm) from the ground and put the wires at about 1 foot (30 cm) intervals. For some plants like clematis, you'll need to make a mesh by weaving thinner galvanised wire vertically through the horizontal wires. It sounds a bit complicated but it's not.

If you want to fix climbers to the house wall, the best way is to fix battens first. Use 1 in × 1½ in (25 mm × 36 mm) roofing laths which you can buy at any builders' merchant. The wooden laths are Rawlplugged and screwed to the wall and the wires can then be stapled to them, again at 1 foot (30 cm) intervals. Using the battens lifts the wires away from the wall and allows the climbers to get behind them to cling on.

The alternative is to use either wooden or plastic trellis which again should be fixed to battens on the wall. I find the wires less obtrusive, but that's just a personal preference.

The third group includes climbing roses and most wall shrubs. These neither twist nor twine so they have to be tied in to the wires, but the same kind of support will do.

For climbers, and particularly wall shrubs that only need occasional fixing, wall nails are useful and available at most garden centres. They're tough masonry nails that will hammer into brickwork, but they have a lead tag on top, which can be wound round the stem to be fixed.

When you're planting climbers, remember that the bottom of a wall or fence can be just about the driest part of the garden. This is especially so against the house wall where the overhang of the eaves prevents rain reaching the ground. So enrich the soil especially well with organic matter to retain what water there is and always plant about 1 foot (30 cm) away from the wall. The plant can be threaded into the wires where it will soon catch hold.

Above. Lead-headed wall nails are a convenient means of fixing some plants to the wall. *Below*. Most climbers can be fixed to the fence with horizontal wires. Strain them tight using a length of wood as a lever against a post.

Herbaceous plants are generally bought in pots these days and can be planted at any time. Bare-rooted plants are best put in during early autumn or spring.

It's also as well to try to prevent as much water loss as possible, by shading the roots with a mulch of organic matter. And (here I go again!) make sure you don't neglect the watering afterwards.

Planting herbaceous perennials

Herbaceous plants are really very accommodating in that they can be shifted at almost any time during the growing season between March and October. As I have already said, if the

worst comes to the worst and you feel you've made a mistake, you can water the plant, move it with a good ball of soil and replant. A good watering afterwards will soon have it looking respectable again, even in the middle of the summer.

But this should be looked on as a last resort and you should endeavour to get the planting done either in early autumn or in the spring.

Again, prepare the soil in advance. You should only need to add peat if the soil is very heavy and difficult to work to a fine consistency. Placing the plants in position before planting will give you a good idea of how they'll look when the border is finished.

Scatter a couple of handfuls of Growmore or rose fertiliser over each square yard to be planted and plant with a trowel, firming in around the plants with your hands. Again, the pots must be watered before planting and the plants must be watered in really well afterwards.

You'll sometimes see it recommended that you plant herbaceous perennials in groups of three or five. Well, that's an expensive way to do it and quite unnecessary. Often you'll find that a single pot will divide into several separate plants. Just knock the plant out of the pot and either pull it apart carefully or cut it into sections with a knife. These pieces can then be planted 6 to 9 inches (15–23 cm) apart where they'll soon form a solid clump much faster than if you planted the whole pot on its own.

There are one or two perennials that really resent being moved – things like hellebores and paeonies like to get their roots down and then stay put. So it's worth checking and then planting these few just a little more carefully to make sure you get them in the right place first time. But on the whole, you'll find it difficult to go wrong with herbaceous plants.

Planting bulbs
Start planting the spring-flowering bulbs in August, just as soon as they become available. The first ones to go in should be daffodils which do need to get an early start. After that you've got until the end of October or even into November to get the rest in.

The prepared borders should need no extra conditioning except for a couple of handfuls of fertiliser over each square yard. But bear in mind that no bulb likes wet conditions. They must all have good drainage and *never* be planted where

A good way to plant bulbs is to dig out a wide hole a little deeper than necessary, put in a layer of grit and then set the bulbs on that.

they'll stand in soaking-wet soil which will quickly rot them. If your soil is heavy, put a good thick layer of coarse grit beneath them.

It's much the best thing to plant bulbs in groups rather than singly and they should never go in ranks like so many disciplined soldiers. I planted ours by digging out a hole about 2 feet (60 cm) wide, putting a layer of grit in the bottom and then setting the bulbs in a circle with one in the middle. That way they help support each other and look less formal.

The important thing is to get them in deeply enough and, unless you intend lifting them after flowering, to put them where they won't get dug up again. Remember that for most of the summer and all the winter, you won't be able to see them at all, so it's easy to make a mistake and dig them up. Ideally, put them fairly near to shrubs which won't be dug around, for fear of damaging the roots.

The depth of planting varies, of course, but, as a rule of thumb, plant about two and a half times deeper then the depth of the bulb itself. There are one or two notable exceptions to this rule, but as most bulbs these days are bought pre-packed, the instructions are sure to be on the back of the pack.

Most summer-flowering bulbs should be planted in spring so that they appear above ground after the danger of hard frosts has passed. There are one or two exceptions, lilies being the most obvious. They can go in during the autumn or again in the early spring.

Hardy annuals

The cheapest way to fill the garden is with hardy annuals grown from seed. Plants like clary, Shirley poppies, love-in-a-mist and Virginia stocks make a wonderful show right from May to the first hard frosts in October or November for the cost of a few packets of seeds.

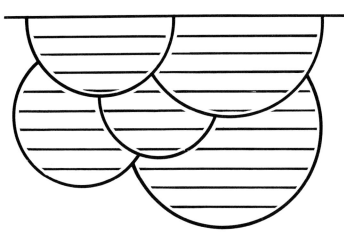

To sow hardy annuals in informal drifts, mark out the drifts first but then sow in straight drills within them. This helps sort the plants from the weeds at thinning time.

They are most valuable plants for the first-timer, not just because they're cheap but also because they can be used to fill in the bare spaces left while you're waiting for the shrubs and herbaceous perennial plants to grow to full size. This way you really can have a superbly colourful garden in the very first season.

They should be sown direct in the open ground in March, or as soon as the soil is dry enough to cultivate a seed-bed. If your soil is heavy, help it along by covering the required areas with a bit of clear polythene in the autumn to keep it dry and to warm it up ready for an early sowing. On really heavy soil, you can also run a little seed compost into drills that have been made a little deeper than normal, to give the seeds a flying start.

Start by marking out the area you want to sow by scratching a line with a stick. Make the areas irregular in shape, to give you informal drifts rather than a series of straight lines. Nonetheless, it's still a good idea to sow the seeds in straight lines within that irregular area. You'll find that weed seedlings will germinate at the same time as the hardy annuals and it's quite difficult to tell which are the weeds and which are the flowers. This way, you'll know that the ones in the straight lines are the ones to keep!

Generally the drills should be about 6 to 8 inches (15–20 cm) apart and as shallow as you can make them. I find it's easier to scratch them with a stick than with the edge of a hoe, which tends to go too deep.

Sow the seeds thinly down the drills and cover by running

the rake down the middle of the rows. Then tap them down lightly with the back of the rake. Once they show through, clean between the rows with a hoe or by hand and, when the seedlings are large enough to handle, thin them out, again generally to 6 to 8 inches (15–20 cm), depending on the size of the plants. The seedlings you pull out won't transplant well, so there's no point in trying – just throw them away.

An alternative method is to sow in seed-trays of soil-less compost, putting them in a fairly shady spot outside. You can also germinate them on the windowsill if you want to get them a little further advanced, but if you do, put them outside in a sheltered spot once they come through. Then, when they're more or less filling the seed-tray, cut them up into squares about 1 in × 1 in (2·5 cm × 2·5 cm) with an old kitchen knife and plant them out 6 to 8 inches (15–20 cm) apart.

Half-hardy annuals and perennials
Generally referred to as 'summer bedding', these showy plants, such as salvias, petunias, lobelia, geraniums and fuchsias, can be used in the same way as hardy annuals, to fill in spaces between shrubs and hardy perennials until they reach full size. Mind you, I wouldn't like to give the impression that this is their *only* use. I would always leave a few permanent spaces to be filled with bedding plants each spring, because they brighten up the borders no end.

Never buy half-hardies until the last frosts have well and truly gone. That means the last week in May for the south of the country, the first week in June for the Midlands and even later in some colder areas further north.

Prepare the soil by lightly forking over the top few inches and, if you can, working in a bit of organic matter and a little fertiliser. I would use Growmore or a rose fertiliser but make sure you don't overdo it. If you use more than about a handful to each square yard (sq. m) you'll get lots of leafy growth at the expense of flowers.

Then it's just a case of carefully removing the whole block of plants from the seed-tray, pulling them apart and planting them one by one. Again I would plant in informal drifts. After planting, it's worth watering in to moisten the soil and to settle it around the roots.

Just one word of warning. Bear in mind that if you're planting just to fill spaces while the permanent plants grow, you must not plant too close to them. If you do that, you'll restrict growth and that rather defeats the object!

TREES

Thankfully the habit seems to have died out now, but in the 1960s and 1970s, there was a fashion for planting weeping willows in the front garden. In those days nurseries and landscape gardeners had a nice little sideline selling the trees to insistent householders and then charging them again to cut them down. After about five years they had to hack their way into the house! If you've got a small garden, you must tailor your trees to suit it.

Most small gardens, of course, will only have room for one, or at most two trees, so they really have to earn their place. What you're looking for is a small tree that will give you at least two cracks of the whip during the year: either a show of flower in spring followed by berries in autumn, or perhaps good variegated foliage colour in summer, turning red, orange or yellow in autumn with, perhaps, the bonus of attractive bark. It sounds a tall order but there are, in fact, dozens of trees that will fill that particular bill.

First of all you should consider fruit trees. These days, apples can be bought on a variety of dwarfing rootstocks, so it's not necessary to have an enormous giant in the back yard. If you only have room for one, you can even buy a 'family tree' which has three varieties on the same plant, thus providing a bit of variety and a built-in pollination service too!

There are also dwarf cherries, plums and even a peach which will suit most small gardens. All these plants will pay the rent by giving an attractive display of flower in spring followed by edible and good-looking fruit in their season.

The vast subject of fruit trees is not for this book, but I would suggest that you get hold of a good fruit specialist's catalogue and find out what's available.

When you buy an ornamental tree, do check that it will suit your conditions. My favourite small tree, the snowy mespilus, for example, would tempt anyone, but unless your soil is acid you may not get good results. And there's nothing more depressing to a keen gardener than the sight of a plant that's obviously unhappy. The following list is short, but gives a good guide to what's available at the garden centre.

Maple (Acer)
Maples vary widely, with some excellent small trees for small

gardens and some that are much too vigorous. The ordinary sycamore, for example, is a maple and although it's a handsome woodland tree, it's out of place in most gardens.

The paperbark maple (*Acer griseum*) is a superb tree for a small plot. Its ascending branches give it a good shape for a restricted space and the foliage is orange-buff in the spring when it first unfolds, turning green and then fiery red in autumn. As an added bonus, the orange bark peels back when it's old to show cinnamon-coloured new bark.

A. 'Flamingo' makes a good small tree, though I would prefer to grow it as a shrub. The foliage opens pink and turns green with a white and pink variegation. But it really needs regular annual trimming to encourage new growth which is much brighter. That's sometimes not easy on a tree, but if you grow it as a shrub you can happily cut it back hard.

The Norway maples (*A. platanoides*) are quite a bit bigger but fine for a medium-sized garden. Most will grow from about 20 to 25 feet (6–7 m) in 10 years. That sounds much bigger than it actually is, so it's not a bad idea to go outside and check the height of a tree (perhaps comparing it to the house, which probably has eaves something like 20 to 25 feet (6–7 m) high, to persuade yourself that you're not buying a monster!

A. 'Drummondii' has striking green foliage with a broad creamy-white margin.

A. 'Royal Red' makes a shapely tree with dark red leaves.

A. 'Brilliantissimum' is a very slow-growing tree suitable for the smallest garden. It's a perfect picture in the spring when the shrimp-pink buds open to bronze-pink leaves. They later turn butter-yellow and then green. A fine tree for its spring show but, in my opinion, a bit of a disappointment afterwards.

The 'golden sycamore' (*A.* 'Worlei') is bigger but it keeps its yellow foliage until July, when it turns a fresh green.

The 'snake-bark maple' (*A. capillipes*) has fresh green leaves which are reddish when young and in the autumn turn bright orange-red. Its most interesting feature is the bark which is green with white streaks on it resembling an exotic snake's skin.

Grey Alder (Alnus incana)
This is a conical tree which grows at least 30 to 40 feet (9–12 m) tall, but I include it in my list because it will grow in cold, wet soil where nothing much else will thrive. It has

greyish leaves with an attractive silver felt underneath. Its smaller brother, *Alnus incana* 'Aurea', has soft yellow young foliage and yellow bark plus red-tinted catkins.

Snowy Mespilus (*Amelanchier lamarckii*)

This is just about my favourite tree but it's just a little bit of a prima donna. It will only do really well on an acid soil. However, I have seen it growing in limy soil, where it reached a height of about 15 feet (4.5 m) and formed a very attractive, spreading shape, so you may consider it worth a try. This one really does earn its living. In early spring it makes a fine, spreading tree with soft bronze foliage with clouds of starry white flowers – they're a real treat after the dull winter, believe me. Later, the leaves turn green and then, in the autumn, rich orange and red. And, as if that were not enough, they also provide edible small black berries in summer.

Birch (*Betula*)

The birches are wonderful for bark colour provided you choose the right variety. Our native silver birch (*Betula pendula*) is a very beautiful tree but not a patch on some of the foreigners which have a delicate tracery of bare branches in winter, striking bark and fresh green foliage all spring and summer. Avoid buying a native silver birch that has been dug bare-rooted unless it has a very good root system. These trees transplant very badly so they stand a better chance of survival if bought in containers.

The white-barked Himalayan birch (*B. jaquemontii*) has just about the whitest stems possible. I know one good gardener who actually polishes his before gardening guests arrive!

The Himalayan birch (*B. utilis*) is similar but probably a little more creamy white.

Katsura Tree (*Cercidiphyllum japonicum*)

Not much of a flowerer but as a foliage plant it's nothing short of magnificent. Buy it as a multi-stemmed tree if you can. The slender stems carry small, heart-shaped leaves which open bright pink, turning sea-green later. Then in the autumn it becomes smoky pink, red and yellow. Quite a sight.

Flowering Thorns (*Crataegus*)

If your soil is a bit heavy, a thorn will serve you well. Thorns grow almost anywhere. They flower in late spring and are at their best in May.

FIRST TIME GARDEN

Right: Norway Maple (*Acer plantanoides*)
Below: Snowy Mespilus (*Amelanchior lamarckii*)
Bottom: Japanese Crab (*Malus floribunda*)

Left: Autumn Cherry (*Prunus subhirtella* 'Rosea')
Below: Mountain Ash (*Sorbus cashmiriana*)
Bottom: Wisteria siniensis

Crataegus oxycantha 'Paul's Double Scarlet Thorn' (also known as 'Coccinea Plena') is rightly the most popular. It forms a small, round-headed tree covered in bright red flowers in May.

Honey Locust (Gleditsia triacanthos 'Sunburst')
A striking, medium-sized, broad-headed tree with bright yellow foliage in spring, turning green with age. It has the small snag that it's one of the latest starters of the season. Nonetheless, a fine tree for a dark corner.

Golden Chains (Laburnum vossii)
A good tree for a small garden in that it has a sharply ascending habit like a triangle tipped upside-down, so you can generally grow plants underneath. The green bark is attractive at all times and in May and June it's smothered in pendulous bunches of bright yellow flowers. The seeds of all laburnums are poisonous so it's perhaps not a good idea if you have one of those small children who insists on eating everything. This particular variety has less seed than most others.

Ornamental Crab (Malus)
Crab apples are marvellous trees for small gardens, with the only difficulty being the choice of the many attractive varieties. They'll all give you a wonderful show of flowers in spring, followed by masses of brightly coloured fruits in late summer and autumn, many of which can be used to make crab-apple jelly. There are lots to choose from and all are good.

The Japanese crab (*Malus floribunda*) is one of the best. Deep red buds open to pale pink and later turn white. Since the flowers open at different times, the tree carries all colours at the same time. The flowers are followed by small, cherry-like fruits.

M. 'Golden Hornet' has white flowers in spring, followed by abundant bright yellow fruits in autumn. The birds leave them until last, so they'll remain on until December.

M. *hupehensis* is one of the most abundant flowerers and fruiters. The flowers are pink in bud, opening to white, and they're scented. The currant-like fruit is yellow flushed red.

M. 'John Downie' is the one to go for if you are keen to make jelly or wine. It has a more upright habit, and the pink-budded, white flowers are followed by large, orange-scarlet fruit.

M. 'Lizet' gives a real colour contrast. Its leaves are deep red, the flowers are blood-red and the fruits deep crimson.

M. 'Profusion' has coppery young foliage later turning green. The purple-red flowers paling to pink are followed by ox-blood red fruits.

M. 'Red Jade' is a small weeping tree with white or blush-pink flowers and bright red fruits.

M. sargentii is one of the smallest of the crabs and ideal for the tiniest garden. Yellow-tinted buds open to white flowers with yellow stamens. The fruits are like bright red currants in late summer and autumn.

Prunus

Flowering almonds, cherries, plums and peaches all belong to this family and all are quite easy to grow. They will do quite well on chalky soil and need very little pruning. They do tend to suffer from the fungus disease peach leaf curl which causes ugly orange blisters on the leaves. Almonds are most prone so I have excluded them from the list.

Purple-leafed Plum (*Prunus cerasifera* 'Nigra') is a wonderful sight in late March and April when the pink flowers contrast well with the blood-red foliage. The leaves later turn deep purple.

P. 'Accolade' is one of the best of the early-flowering cherries. It has an open, spreading habit and the branches are covered in deep pink buds which open to semi-double light pink flowers with pretty, fringed petals. It flowers in early April and continues for a long period.

Sargent's Cherry (*P. sargentii*) is a shapely small tree with clouds of single pink flowers in early spring. The leaves open coppery red and later turn green, colouring to brilliant vermillion and crimson in autumn. Well worth its place.

Tibetan Cherry (*P. serrula*) is a slightly larger tree with masses of white flowers in May. Its main attraction is its mahogany-red bark which peels away to show a brightly polished surface.

The Autumn Cherry (*P. subhirtella* 'Autumnalis') is a small tree with semi-double white flowers produced intermittently from November to March. The variety 'Rosea' has pink flowers.

Right: Clematis alpina
Below: Honeysuckle (*Lonicera periclymenum* 'Belgica')

Left: Albertine rose
Below: Virginia Creeper
(*Parthenocissus henryana*)

P. 'Kanzan' is the best-known double-flowering cherry. It has enormous clusters of large, deep pink flowers in spring, contrasting well with its bronze foliage which later turns green.

Cheal's Weeping Cherry is a small, weeping tree with clusters of rose-pink flowers in spring.

Willow-leafed Pear (Pyrus salicifolia 'Pendula')
A weeping tree with silvery-grey, willow-like leaves. It has white flowers in April but is grown mainly for its foliage. The fruit is not edible.

Golden Acacia (Robinia pseudoacacia 'Frisia')
An outstanding small tree with butter-yellow foliage throughout the season. Unfortunately it tends to suffer a little from die-back and it resents a windy spot. It is not a good mover, so buy it in a container.

Kilmarnock Willow (Salix caprea 'Pendula')
A good weeping willow for a small garden. Unlike its big brother, it won't take over! It forms a small, umbrella-shaped tree which carries white catkins in late winter which open to bright, golden yellow in spring.

Mountain Ashes and Whitebeams (Sorbus)
This is another big family many of whose members will earn their place in the small garden because they produce good flowers and berries of various colours in the autumn. In my experience, the birds prefer the red-berried varieties and will leave the yellow and white ones until later in the season.

The Rowan or Mountain Ash (*Sorbus aucuparia*) is the best known and a British native. This one forms a small, round-headed tree with white spring flowers followed by yellow berries which quickly turn orange and then red.

S. cashmiriana is a superb, open tree with ferny foliage turning red in autumn. The pink flowers are freely borne in May, followed by glistening white berries.

S. 'Joseph Rock' has white flowers in spring, followed by yellow berries. There is good autumn foliage colour.

S. sargentiana is a magnificent small-garden tree. The winter buds are large and sticky like a horse-chestnut, but crimson. The leaves are large and very attractive, turning red in autumn, while the small fruits are bright red and borne in large clusters.

Whitebeam (*S. aria* 'Lutescens') is a striking tree in spring when the leaves are bright silver. They later turn grey. *S. aria* 'Mitchellii' is like the ordinary whitebeam but with much larger, more dramatic leaves.

Climbers and wall shrubs

When your fences are first put up they will look a bit stark. Certainly they'll accentuate the limited size of the garden but, though they may at that stage seem like a necessary evil as they provide protection and privacy, they are, in fact, a valuable asset. They are the modern equivalent of the stone or brick walls of the old 'stately-home' gardens which were much prized in their day.

Look upon them as supports for plants which will, because they face different directions, actually provide four different sets of conditions for four different sets of plants. You'll have the interest of growing a whole range of climbing plants and wall shrubs, most of which are very fast-growing and will quickly transform your fences. What's more, they take up virtually no garden room at all, while giving you more or less instant height and masses of colour.

Perhaps you should first decide whether or not to use your fences largely as productive areas for fruit. You could, for example, grow peaches, apricots, figs and nectarines on the fence that faces south, pears on the west-facing one, apples and plums to the east and acid cherries and quinces on the north. All can be trained in attractive fan shapes and all have flowers and, of course, fruits that are worth looking at.

But even if you do decide to use parts of the fencing to grow fruit, let me try to persuade you to grow other, purely decorative climbers too. They'll give you such a marvellous show over such a long period that they really are a joy.

But you don't have to restrict the climbers to the fences. They can also be grown through trees to give an extra show of flowers, they can be allowed to scramble over shrubs in the borders or they can be used as ground-coverers too.

If you're going to use them in this way, it's important to choose carefully. It would be folly, for example, to grow one of the most vigorous clematis or the rampant Russian vine through a small tree because either plant would simply swamp the tree.

When choosing climbers, you'll need to take several points into consideration. The most important is the aspect. While most climbers will do well on the warmest south-facing fence, the choice is more restricted for north and east-facing positions.

Then consider how the plants are going to be supported. If, for example, you're clothing the house wall, you may prefer a self-clinger like ivy or Virginia creeper, which will do away with the need to fix wires to the wall. If you're prepared to provide a trellis or a series of wires as support, you can grow those plants that support themselves by twining, like honeysuckle, or by clinging on, like clematis. Some, of course, like roses, do neither and they must have a framework on which they can be tied.

Wall shrubs are a different kettle of fish. They don't exactly climb and certainly won't cling on or twine. But they do have a stiff, upright habit of growth that makes them suitable for the purpose. Many are, in fact plants that, in the wild, lie prostrate, often over rocks, where they benefit from the reflected warmth. When grown against a wall, they tend to do the same only in a perpendicular position. A perfect example of this phenomenon is the herringbone cotoneaster, *Cotoneaster horizontalis*.

It's also important to choose a plant of the correct vigour. Plants like Russian vine or some of the more vigorous kinds of clematis are fine for hiding an oil tank or an ugly outhouse but they are too rampant for most other purposes.

Plants for north and east-facing walls

Flowering Quince (Chaenomeles varieties)
Just to complicate matters, these are sometimes called 'Cydonia' and often just 'Japonica'. They are very stiff in growth and always give plenty of flower of different colours, depending on variety, from deep red, through pink to white. The flowers are followed by large, highly-coloured fruits. In the early years they need no support but later they may need to be held back with a few lead-headed nails.

Clematis
There are numerous sorts that will do well against a north or

east-facing wall. It's generally the pink-flowered ones that are grown in these situations as they are then less prone to fading. The large-flowered garden hybrids have big, trumpet-shaped flowers while the species have smaller flowers. Some of the latter have thick-petalled yellow flowers while others are a delicate nodding pink and blue. Beware of the really vigorous types like *Clematis montana* and its varieties which may be too rampant. All clematis need supporting on wire mesh or trellis.

Herringbone Cotoneaster (*Cotoneaster horizontalis*)
A neat plant notable for the way its side-shoots come out of the main stems in a perfectly regular pattern, just like a herringbone. It has small white flowers in spring followed by bright red berries. Very striking but will only grow 5 to 6 feet (150–180 cm) high. They need no support.

Silk Tassel Bush (*Garrya elliptica*)
The male plant is a magnificent evergreen with long, drooping tassels of grey-green catkins in January and February. It is better, in my view, than the female, though many gardeners prefer the long clusters of deep purple-brown fruits. Support with wall nails or horizontal wires.

Ivy (*Hedera*)
There are many different ivies, some with brightly variegated leaves. They are all self-clinging so need no support. Don't expect the existing growths to stick to the fence. It's only the new ones that will do so as they grow. Most are slow-growing until they do get attached and then go away quite quickly.

Climbing Hydrangea (*Hydrangea petiolaris*)
Another self-clinger, with large leaves and flat plates of pretty white flowers in June. Fast-growing once it gets attached and will grow up to about 75 feet (23 m) high.

Honeysuckle (*Lonicera*)
Most honeysuckles flower best in full sun but a few do well in shade. *Lonicera americana* is a free-flowerer with long, fragrant blooms starting white and fading to deep yellow with a purple back. The Japanese honeysuckle (*L. japonica*) has a variety 'Aureo-reticulata' which is grown for its neat, bright green leaves with a conspicuous yellow veining.

Virginia Creeper (Parthenocissus quinquefolia)
A self-clinger with glossy green leaves all summer, turning brilliant red-purple in autumn. Not an evergreen. If you can find it, grow its near relative *Parthenocissus henryana*, which has leaves prettily veined white.

Russian Vine (Polygonum baldschuanicum)
A rampant, twining climber, useful for covering unsightly objects. But make sure the outhouse you grow it over is strong. I have seen this plant pull down an old building! It bears clouds of white flowers tinged with pink.

Firethorn (Pyracantha)
This is a stiff, thorny plant with superb glossy foliage and masses of white flowers in spring. It is generally covered in berries in autumn and these vary in colour from yellow to bright orange and red, depending on variety. Best supported with horizontal wires or wall nails.

Rose
Climbing and rambling roses can be grown against just about any fence or wall. The main difference is that ramblers are generally more vigorous and flower once or twice a season, while climbers are less vigorous and often perpetual flowering. They are, of course, not evergreen. There are dozens and dozens of good varieties to choose from in every colour of the rainbow. They need to be supported by tying the branches into horizontal wires or twisting them through trellis.

Vines (Vitis)
One of the most popular vine varieties is 'Brandt' (sometimes spelt Brant), which is a vigorous climber producing numerous bunches of small, sweet, red grapes. It has the added advantage that the leaves turn deep red-purple in autumn. *Vitis coignetiae* is one of the most spectacular with enormous heart-shaped leaves which turn purple in autumn. Vines need the support of horizontal wires.

Plants for south and west-facing walls

Kiwi Fruit or Chinese Gooseberry (Actinidia chinensis)
A vigorous plant with hairy red shoots and large, heart-shaped leaves. It bears white flowers in late summer but they are not striking. It will occasionally produce fruit outside, but only if male and female forms are planted together.

Californian Lilac (Ceanothus)
There are several kinds to choose from, most of which have lots of flowers in varying shades of blue. Some lose their leaves but the evergreen types are much the best for covering walls and fences. They are stiffly upright but need some support from wires or wall nails.

Wintersweet (Chimonanthus praecox)
A wall shrub with sweetly scented, waxy-yellow flowers with a central purple blotch. They have the great advantage of flowering in winter and very early spring.

Clematis
There are dozens of excellent varieties of this most popular climber of all. Basically, there are two types to choose from – the large, trumpet-flowered hybrids like the pale blue 'Mrs Cholmondeley', the rose-pink 'Comtesse de Bouchard' or the petunia-red 'Ernest Markham' and the smaller-flowered species like the lovely violet, red or purple-flowered *Clematis viticella* or the blue *C. alpina*.

All varieties of clematis will do well on the warmer south and west-facing walls. But though they prefer to have their heads in the sun, they do like a cool, moist root-run, so it's essential to shade the root area after planting. This can be done by covering the soil with a paving slab or two, by mulching with gravel or chipped bark, or by growing a spreading plant over the area.

Clematis tend to suffer from a disease called 'clematis wilt'. It's a fungus which causes the plant to wilt from the top downwards. It can be controlled by cutting back below the wilted part as soon as you see it and then spraying with benomyl (Benlate). But sometimes this is not enough and the plant has to be cut right down to ground level. So, just in case it does strike, always plant clematis deeply, so that the top of the pot is covered by about 6 inches (15 cm) of soil. The fungus won't attack below soil level so you'll always have plenty of new young shoots to come.

Before you buy, just check with the garden centre that the variety is not too vigorous for your needs. The large-flowered varieties like 'Jackmanii Superba', 'Ville de Lyon' and 'Nellie Moser' are never going to cause problems, but the smaller-flowered species like *C. montana* or *C. tangutica* could take over.

Clematis cling on by twisting their leaf-stalks around the

supports, so they need a mesh to cover the wall well. If you just use horizontal wires, they'll travel along the wall but fail to go up it. So you'll have to thread thinner galvanised wire vertically through the horizontal wires to make a square mesh. Alternatively, fix a wooden or plastic trellis to the wall.

Chilean Glory Flower (*Eccremocarpus scaber*)
This climber is unusual in that it can be raised quite easily from seed sown on the windowsill in early spring. Although it's a perennial, it will get cut down by frost in all but the warmest areas, so there's nothing to see in the winter. But, if you protect the roots by throwing a couple of handfuls of strawy manure or similar material over the top of the soil in the autumn, it'll show up again in spring to cover your fence with delightful orange-red, tubular bells. Support it with wire mesh or trellis.

Sweetspire (*Itea ilicifolia*)
A jolly useful shrub in that it's evergreen and there aren't that many of those suitable for growing up the fence. It looks a bit like holly but in late summer it's loaded with long, whitish-green catkins. Support it with horizontal wires or wall nails.

Honeysuckle (*Lonicera*)
Most honeysuckles will do well on a south or west-facing wall. I don't think you can beat our native woodbine (*Lonicera periclymenum*) which has sweetly fragrant flowers, creamy white within and purplish outside. It flowers from June to September and then follows with red berries. I would also recommend two popular varieties, 'Belgica' or 'Early Dutch', which has reddish-purple flowers fading to yellow during May and June and again in late summer, and the 'Late Dutch' or 'Serotina', which is much the same but flowers later. Look out also for 'Dropmore Scarlet' which has bright red flowers from July to October.

Wisteria
A well-known and popular climber with long trusses of blue flowers in May and June.

BORDERS

The sunny border

There's no doubt that the easiest of all borders to plant is the one that gets full sun for at least part of the day. The range of plants for this kind of spot is virtually endless. But it could still have its share of headaches, especially if the soil is light and sandy.

To prevent problems of drying out in hot weather, it pays to prepare the border well by adding as much organic matter as you can afford at the outset and topping up regularly every year. After the first year you'll at least have some home-made compost to use, so it won't be quite such an expensive job. Use extra organic matter every time you plant a new bit of border. When it's all planted you naturally won't be able to dig it in, but if you lightly fork over the top couple of inches (5 cm) each autumn or spring and then add as thick a mulch of compost, manure, peat or bark as you can, the worms will soon take it down to the lower regions where it'll do most good. That way you'll also prevent evaporation of surface moisture and you'll save yourself a lot of weeding too.

Even with these precautions, you may still find that in a hot, dry summer you have to water. If you do, make sure you do so with a hose and preferably a lawn sprinkler, putting it on for at least an hour at a time. If you sprinkle a little on the top from a can, you encourage the young roots up to the surface where they'll suffer even more if they dry out.

Shrubs for full sun

Southernwood (Artemisia)
There are several shrubby and herbaceous artemisias, all of which are good in a dry, sunny spot. Indeed, as a general rule you could bet that if a plant has silver or grey leaves it will do well in sunshine. They are all grown for the beauty of their silver foliage.

Barberry (Berberis)
This is a large family of shrubs, all of which will do well in sun and on heavy soil too. They have orange or yellow flowers and the deciduous types are prized for their berries and brilliant autumn foliage.

Butterfly Bush (Buddleia davidii)
This is a fast-growing, medium-sized shrub with large heads of blossom that are white, red, purple or blue according to variety. They attract butterflies by the hundred.

Caryopteris clandonensis
A small, showy shrub with grey-green, aromatic foliage and blue flower spikes in late summer.

Californian Lilac (Ceanothus)
Medium to large-sized shrubs, and some kinds are evergreen. All have superb blue flowers in summer. Some are a little too tender for northern gardens.

Sun Rose (Cistus)
You must be careful to choose the hardier varieties if you live further north, but these showy plants are well worth trying because of their sheer volume of flower. Most are white but there are a few lilac, crimson, purple and yellow-marked varieties. They make small, rounded bushes and do well on chalk.

Cotoneaster
Another big family, most of which will do well in a wide variety of soils and situations. Some are deciduous but others are evergreen or semi-evergreen, losing their leaves in hard winters. They vary from prostrate ground-coverers to medium-sized shrubs. The deciduous types are noted for their autumn foliage colour. All have white or pink-tinged flowers in June and many follow these with a good crop of red or orange berries.

Broom (Cytisus)
A large family of green-stemmed shrubs, ranging from prostrate types to very large plants. They are very free-flowering indeed and available in a range of colours and bicolours.

Escallonia
Valuable evergreens, growing generally into medium to large-sized shrubs. They have small, shiny leaves and small flowers in various shades of white, pink, crimson and red in late summer or early autumn. Not all are entirely hardy, though they do well in seaside gardens.

Spindle (Euonymus)
The evergreen types, like *Euonymus fortunei* 'Emerald and Gold' and 'Emerald Gaiety', make excellent ground-cover evergreens with variegated leaves of green and gold or green and cream.

Genista
Yellow-flowered shrubs closely related to brooms. They range from dwarf to medium-sized shrubs and all are tolerant of most types of garden soil.

Shrubby Veronica (Hebe)
The shrubby veronicas are a large and varied group, evergreen and tolerant of most garden soils. Not all are hardy, so choose with care. Most form small to medium-sized shrubs with white or sometimes rich-blue flowers. There are also some varieties called 'whipcord' hebes which look a little bit like a conifer with olive-green stems shaded yellow.

Hibiscus
Beautiful late-flowering shrubs with trumpet-shaped flowers of pink, white, red, lilac, purple and blue according to variety, like small hollyhocks.

Hypericum
The low-growing *Hypericum calycinum* (rose of Sharon) should only be grown where its invasive nature will not become a nuisance. However, there are several small to medium-sized shrubs that are ideally suited to a small garden, perhaps the most commonly grown being *H. patulum* 'Hidcote'. All hypericums bear masses of saucer-shaped, single yellow flowers for most of the summer and autumn.

Beauty Bush (Kolkwitzia amabilis)
An easily-grown, medium-sized shrub, covered in clouds of pink flowers in May and June.

Lavender (Lavandula)
Small, silver-leafed, aromatic shrubs with fragrant blue flowers from July to September.

Mock Orange (Philadelphus)
Easily-grown, medium to large, sweetly scented flowering shrubs. The flowers are generally white, sometimes with pink

or yellow shading. *Philadelphus coronarius* 'Aureus' has bright golden foliage.

Cinquefoil (Potentilla)
Small to medium-sized shrubs with mostly yellow flowers over a long period. Look out for some of the newer, coloured varieties like the blush-pink 'Daydawn' and the vermillion 'Red Ace'.

Stag's Horn Sumach (Rhus typhina)
A large shrub or small tree with felted brown bark and deeply toothed leaves which colour bright red in autumn. It also bears large brown 'cones' late in the season. It has the disadvantage of suckering but is not too difficult to control.

Flowering Currant (Ribes sanguineum)
A popular easily-grown, medium-sized shrub with generally pink or red pendulous flowers in spring and early summer.

Roses
All types of roses will do well in a sunny spot. Bush roses generally grow from 2 to 5 feet (60–150 cm) though there are a few very vigorous varieties. There are two types – hybrid teas, which have fewer, well-shaped blooms, and floribundas, which carry more blooms of a less perfect shape. In other words, hybrid teas are for viewing close-up or for cutting, while floribundas make a fine mass display. There are several other types that deserve a place in the cottage garden border. 'English' roses have been bred to have the old-fashioned type of flower but with the added advantage of being perpetual flowering. 'Shrub' roses are hybrids between species and old-fashioned roses. Many have the advantage of wonderful blooms which are nearly always very fragrant, along with striking red or orange hips in autumn. Most flower over a much shorter period than the modern roses. Some shrub roses are very vigorous, so check the eventual height and spread before you buy. The newer miniature roses are ideal for the small garden.

Rosemary (Rosmarinus officinalis)
A dense, aromatic, medium-sized shrub with blue flowers in May.

Cotton Lavender (Santolina chamaecyparissus)
A small shrub with silver foliage and sulphur-yellow flowers.

Senecio greyi
A popular small shrub forming a dense mound of silver-grey foliage topped by yellow daisies in summer.

Spanish Broom (Spartium junceum)
A strong-growing, large shrub with thick, rush-like green stems and large, fragrant, pea-like yellow flowers throughout summer and early autumn.

Spiraea
Small to medium-sized shrubs with flattish heads of small flowers. Look out for the bridal wreath plant (*Spiraea arguta*), which is covered in a foam of white flowers in April-May, and S. *bumalda* varieties, such as 'Goldflame', which is grown for its red and gold young foliage that eventually turns yellow, and 'Anthony Waterer', which has flat heads of carmine flowers in summer.

Yucca filamentosa
The spiky heads of this plant give a tropical foliage effect to the border.

Herbaceous perennials
A much cheaper way to fill up your borders, though bear in mind that most die down in winter, leaving bare soil. Again, the list for sunny places is endless.

Bear's Britches (Acanthus spinosus)
A handsome foliage plant with large, leathery, divided leaves and spires of soft mauve, foxglove-like flowers. Will also grow in shade but does not flower so well there.

Yarrow (Achillea)
Medium-sized plants with feathery foliage and flat heads of generally yellow flowers though now there are several new hybrids of various colours.

African Lily (Agapanthus)
A plant blooming in late summer. It has large heads of beautiful blue or white flowers. The garden hybrids 'Bressingham Blue' and 'Bressingham White' are recommended.

Princess Lily (Alstroemeria hybrids)
Long-flowering, medium-sized plants with exotic flowers

resembling the orchid. The newer hybrids are expensive but worth growing since they flower most of the summer.

Pearly Everlasting (Anaphalis triplinervis)
A grey-leafed plant for the front of the border. The white, yellow-tinged flowers are excellent for cutting and drying.

Anchusa azurea
A tall perennial with blue flowers in early summer. Look out for the varieties 'Loddon Royalist', which is gentian blue, and the lighter blue 'Opal'.

Golden Marguerite (Anthemis tinctoria)
A showy plant for near the back of the border. The foliage is parsley-like and topped by sheaves of bright yellow daisies for a long period in summer.

Southernwood (Artemisia)
Like the shrubs, the herbaceous perennials are grown mainly for their silver foliage.

Michaelmas Daisy (Aster)
Well-known perennials with daisy flowers in a variety of colours. Most will grow from 1 to 3 feet (30–90 cm) tall though there are some bigger varieties.

Elephant's Ears (Bergenia)
Excellent ground-cover evergreens. They are worth growing for the leaves alone but they also bear striking flowers in spring. They will do well in shade as well but if grown in full sun, the foliage turns bronze red in winter. Look out for the hybrids 'Ballawley', which has crimson flowers, 'Margery Fish', which is magenta-purple and the pure white 'Silberlicht'.

Bellflower (Campanula)
A big family and most of them are well worth growing. They generally bear cup-shaped flowers in shades of blue, pink and white. Look out especially for the blue or white *Campanula carpatica*, which is ideal for the front of the border, the 5-foot (150 cm) tall *C. lactiflora*, the slightly shorter, blue, white, purple or lilac *C. latifolia* and the 3-foot (90 cm) tall *C. persicifolia*, which has lilac or white flowers. The chimney bellflower, *C. pyramidalis*, forms a 5-foot (90 cm) pyramid covered in cool blue or white flowers in summer.

Cornflower (Centaurea dealbata)
An easy plant to grow, though it will generally need staking. The lilac-pink flowers are carried on 3-foot (90 cm) stems.

Valerian (Centranthus ruber)
A very easy plant which often naturalises itself so could become a nuisance. The 2- to 3-foot (60–90 cm) plants bear long heads of deep pink or white flowers.

Shasta Daisy (Chrysanthemum maximum)
A medium-sized, clump-forming plant that unfailingly produces masses of large white daisies in summer. Look out for the smaller 'Snowcap' for the front of the border.

Tickseed (Coreopsis verticillata)
A dense, upright plant about 2 feet (60 cm) tall with attractive divided foliage. It is covered all summer and autumn with yellow daisies.

Crambe cordifolia
An enormous plant up to about 6 feet (180 cm) tall bearing huge clouds of tiny white flowers in early summer.

Crocosmia hybrids
Bulbous hardy perennials with upright, iris-like foliage and abundant blossoms of red or orange in late summer. Recommended is 'Lucifer', which is a fiery red. They grow to about 3 feet (90 cm).

Delphinium hybrids
Well-known perennials producing tall, stately spikes of blue, purple, pink and white. Slugs love them but, if you can keep them at bay in the early stages, they're perfect for the back of the border.

Border Pink (Dianthus)
The perfect front to a border, these sweetly scented, carnation-type flowers of pink, white, red and maroon are a 'must'.

Globe Thistle (Echinops ritro)
Statuesque plants about 3 to 4 feet (90–120 cm) tall, with attractive thistle-like foliage and globe-shaped flowers of steely blue in late summer.

Right: Beauty Bush (*Kolkwitzia amabilis*)
Below: Broom (*Cytisus praecox*)
Bottom right: Shooting Star (*Dodecatheon maedia*)
Bottom: *Rhododendron yakushimanum*

Foxtail Lily (Eremurus bungei)
Imposing, 4- to 5-foot (120–150 cm) tall plants with strap-shaped leaves and heads of golden flowers with orange anthers in June.

Fleabane (Erigeron hybrids)
Like miniature Michaelmas daisies, these plants come in a variety of colours and are ideal for the front of the border.

Sea Holly (Eryngium oliverianum)
A stately plant about $2\frac{1}{2}$ feet (75 cm) tall, with deeply cut leaves on stout, blue-tinted stems, topped by 'thimbles' of steely blue flowers in summer. Look out also for *Eryngium variifolium*, which forms rosettes of white-veined leaves.

Spurge (Euphorbia)
A large group of plants all of which grow in sun or partial shade. They are all good, but especially so are *Euphorbia griffithii*, which is 2 feet (60 cm) tall and has flame-coloured heads of flowers, *E. myrsinites*, with trailing stems bearing lime-green flowers fading to pink, *E. polychroma (E. epithymoides)* which is about 18 inches (45 cm) tall and has sulphur-yellow flowers on round mounds of fresh green foliage, *E. robbiae*, which grows to 3 feet (90 cm) and has showy greenish-yellow flowers, and *E. wulfenii*, with bluish foliage and greenish-yellow flowers. They all flower in early summer.

Cranesbill (Geranium)
All are easy to grow and make good ground-cover plants though some can be a bit invasive. They vary in colour from blue through lilac to pink and white and many have good autumn leaf-colour too. Excellent under trees.

Avens (Geum chiloense)
Easily-grown, clump-forming plants about 18 inches (45 cm) tall and bearing strongly coloured rosettes of various colours. Look out for 'Lady Stratheden', which has strong yellow flowers, and 'Mrs Bradshaw', which is brick-red. They flower from June to August.

Baby's Breath (Gypsophylla paniculata)
Despite its twee common name, this is an excellent plant, forming hummocks of foliage topped by a mass of tiny, white, star-shaped flowers from August to September. 'Bristol Fairy' is the best white, while 'Rosy Veil' is pink-tinged.

Iris
All irises grow best in full sun but most need a moist situation without it being a wet one or badly drained. The most popular are the 'bearded irises' (*Iris germanica*), which have flowers of various colours, generally bicoloured. They grow 2 to 3 feet (60–90 cm) tall and unfailingly flower in June. Excellent value. There are dwarf bearded irises that otherwise look much the same.

Red Hot Poker (Kniphophia hybrids)
These make clumps of grassy foliage from which arise the 'pokers', about 4 feet (120 cm) tall, of orange, yellow or red in summer. Look out also for 'Green Jade', which has green spikes with a hint of cream. There are also dwarf varieties.

Catmint (Nepeta mussinii)
A greyish, small-leaved plant for the front of the border. It produces masses of lavender flowers from June until autumn. Cats love them.

Oriental Poppy (Papaver orientale)
This poppy forms medium-sized plants bearing superb large richly coloured blooms in shades of red, pink, white or orange. They have a tendency to flop and to lose their foliage by mid-summer, so plant something like baby's breath next to it to take over when it has finished.

Bearded Tongue (Penstemon barbatus)
From a basal tuft of foliage spring numerous scarlet tubular flowers in summer. It grows to about 3 feet (90 cm).

Phlox paniculata hybrids
Superbly showy perennials growing to about 3 feet (90 cm) and producing large pyramids of flower in various shades of red, pink and white from July to September.

Cinquefoil (Potentilla hybrids)
Vigorously spreading plants growing to about $1\frac{1}{2}$ feet (45 cm) and producing masses of brilliant blooms all summer. Especially good are 'Gibson's Scarlet' and 'William Rollison'.

Bouncing Bette (Saponaria ocymoides)
A splendid, low-growing ground-coverer bearing sheets of deep-pink flowers in May and June.

Scabious (Scabiosa caucasica)
One of the best of cut-flowers, this perennial grows to about
2 feet (60 cm) and bears blue or white heads of quality blooms
from July to September.

Ice Plant (Sedum spectabile)
Fleshy-leaved plants growing to about $1\frac{1}{2}$ feet (45 cm) and
bearing flat heads of red or carmine-pink flowers in late
summer. They unfailingly attract hundreds of butterflies.

Thyme (Thymus serpyllum)
A well-known creeping plant for the front of the border. It
bears masses of tiny white or pink flowers over a long period
in summer.

Mullein (Verbascum)
Several mulleins are biennials but there are some reliable
perennials bearing yellow, purple, pink or white flowers
according to variety. Of particular merit are *Verbascum
vernale*, which grows to 6 feet (180 cm) and bears great spikes
of vivid yellow from a basal clump of grey, woolly leaves,
and *V. phoeniceum*, also known as the purple mullein, which
grows to 4 feet (120 cm) and varies from pink to purple.

As you can imagine, this is by no means a complete list of
plants that will grow in a sunny spot, but it will give you a
good start!

Remember to leave spaces, too, for annual and biennial
bedding plants and bulbs, nearly all of which will do well in
sunny conditions.

The moist, shady border
New gardeners often despair when they're faced with a garden
in shade. But really it's quite an enviable position to be in –
provided the ground holds a certain amount of moisture.
There are hundreds of plants that will do very well in those
conditions and many of them are very choice indeed. Generally it's true to say that colours are more subdued, but those
greens, creams, soft blues and pinks really do give a very
restful effect.

As with any border, it's necessary to pay attention to soil
preparation before planting. Though a soil that can hold
water will greatly increase the range of plants you can grow
in it, very few plants like badly drained conditions. So if the

soil is waterlogged, dig in plenty of coarse grit to lighten it and raise the borders somewhat to increase drainage.

The plants I will suggest you grow tend to like semi-shaded conditions. That means that they'll shrivel up if they are subjected to strong sunshine for too long, but they resent really gloomy conditions. So if the shade in your garden comes from large trees, you may find it pays to thin out the odd branch here and there just to let in a little dappled sunshine. There's no need to overdo it though.

Shrubs for shaded borders

Japanese Maple (Acer palmatum)
This is a marvellous foliage shrub that will do well in semi-shade in a sheltered position. It has lovely, sycamore-shaped leaves of vivid green when young. There is also a rich purple-leafed variety. The cut-leafed variety 'Dissectum' is very delicate in foliage and forms a superb, gnarled and twisted little tree in time, but it must have an acid soil and be out of the wind.

Spotted Laurel (Aucuba japonica)
A good evergreen foliage shrub with green leaves spotted yellow. Some of the more modern varieties are more striking in their colouring. It will slowly grow to 6 to 8 feet (180–240 cm).

Camellia
A superb, glossy-leafed, medium-sized evergreen bearing exotic-looking flowers of white, red or pink. It needs an acid soil and should be planted in a position where the early morning sun will not touch frosted buds as this will make them fall prematurely.

Dogwood (Cornus)
Some dogwoods are grown for their winter bark colour, though some also have fine foliage throughout the season and excellent autumn colour too. Prune back hard each spring if grown for bark colour since the young shoots have the most vivid bark.

Castor Oil Plant (Fatsia japonica)
This glossy evergreen foliage plant is often grown as a houseplant yet is generally hardy in sheltered positions.

Checkerberry (Gaultheria procumbens)
A creeping evergreen, forming carpets of dark green leaves with white flowers in spring and bright red berries in autumn and winter.

Witch Hazel (Hamamelis)
Tall shrubs bearing dozens of small, spidery flowers all the way up their stems in winter and early spring. Recommended are *Hamamelis mollis* 'Pallida', with bright yellow flowers, and the orange-red hybrid 'Jelena'.

Ivy (Hedera)
Ivies can be used as wall plants, as recommended on page 153, but they also make good ground cover, forming mats of green or variegated foliage.

Hydrangea
Apart from the well-known 'mop-head' hydrangeas, there are others, like the lovely 'lacecaps' that are worth looking for. They grow into medium to large-sized shrubs and will flower regularly once established. Most flowers are white or pink but some varieties will produce blue flowers on acid soils.

Pieris
If you have an acid soil, then you *must* grow one of these beautiful shrubs. They form medium-sized plants with glossy evergreen foliage. During winter, the red-tinged flower buds are most attractive and they eventually open out in April to pendulous, white, lily-of-the-valley flowers. They are accompanied by the young growths which, on varieties like 'Forest Flame', are bright red.

Rhododendron and Azalea
An acid soil is essential for these shrubs.

Rhododendrons come in a whole variety of sizes and colours. They are all evergreen and have exotic blooms, generally in spring. For a small garden, probably the best are the new *yakushimanum* hydrids. These come from Japan and form small, dome-shaped bushes that are unfailingly covered in spring with flowers of various colours according to variety.

Azaleas are closely related but here there are evergreen and deciduous types. The evergreens are much like miniature rhododendrons, while the deciduous ones have brilliant flowers plus vivid autumn foliage colour. If you don't have an acid soil you can grow them in a peaty compost in a tub, but you must water them with rain water.

Bramble (*Rubus*)

One member of the *Rubus* family, *R. tricolor*, should be avoided in a small garden because it is too invasive. Some types, though, form large shrubs which will not take over. *Rubus cockburnianus* grows to about 8 feet (240 cm) and sports long, arching branches that look as if they've been whitewashed! The flowers are insignificant but the ferny leaves are attractive. *R. tridel* 'Benenden' also makes a vigorous shrub but here the flowers are well worth while. They are pure white with a golden centre and produced all along the arching branches in May.

Willow (*Salix*)

All the small willows are worth while and will not form enormous trees. Look out for plants like *Salix boydii*, which is very small and makes a gnarled and twisted shrub with grey foliage. *S. eleagnos*, the hoary willow, makes a medium to large-sized shrub with red-brown stems and white-felted leaves. The woolly willow (*S. lanata*) makes a small mound with grey leaves and white, then yellow catkins in spring.

Golden Elder (*Sambucus nigra 'Aurea'*)

A relative of our common elder, this makes a medium to large-sized shrub with highly attractive yellow foliage. One of the best golden foliage shrubs.

Christmas Box (*Sarcococca humilis*)

A dwarf shrub with shiny, evergreen leaves and small, highly fragrant white flowers in winter.

Skimmia

Slow-growing, easy, aromatic shrubs of great value in the shade border. The flowers are generally white but look out particularly for 'Kew Green', which has green buds all winter opening to white flowers in spring, and 'Rubella', which has red buds opening to white flowers with yellow anthers.

Snowberry (*Symphoricarpos*)

These are dense shrubs growing to about 4 feet (120 cm) tall. Their flowers are insignificant but they are grown for their large crops of white, red or pink berries in autumn and winter.

Viburnum
Another very large group, several of which will do well in shade. *Viburnum davidii* forms a small, dome-shaped evergreen bush. Its white flowers are borne in June and these are often followed by striking, egg-shaped turquoise fruits. But you do need to plant a few bushes together to make sure of cross-pollination. The guelder rose (*V. opulus*) will grow well in wet situations. The white flowers are very showy, resembling a lacecap hydrangea, and some varieties carry heavy crops of translucent red or yellow berries in autumn. These make quite large shrubs.

Herbaceous perennials
Leave plenty of space for herbaceous plants because there are many really good ones.

Monkshood (Aconitum)
These are tall perennials with hooded flowers, hence the name. Look out for *Aconitum carmichaelii* 'Arendsii', which has deep blue flowers and grows to about 4 feet (120 cm), *A. septentrionale* 'Ivorine', which carries ivory-white blooms and grows a little shorter at about $2\frac{1}{2}$ feet (75 cm) and *A. orientale*, which looks like a delphinium with creamy yellow flowers.

Lady's Mantle (Alchemilla mollis)
The downy, rounded green leaves alone make this plant well worth growing, but it also sports sprays of lime-green flowers in June. It will spread easily and grows to about $1\frac{1}{2}$ feet (45 cm).

Columbine (Aquilegia)
Marvellous, delicate herbaceous plants available in many colours. The most popular are the *Aquilegia vulgaris* hybrids, which have a pronounced spur at the back of the flower. The colours range from yellow to pink, blood-red, purple and white.

Astilbe
Very decorative plants worth growing for their ferny, divided foliage alone. They bear plumes of flowers of many shades of white, pink and red. The garden hybrids are the best bet and these grow 2 to 3 feet (60–90 cm) tall.

Masterwort (Astrantia major)
The flowers of this exquisite plant look for all the world like

old-fashioned posies. They are cream with a green tip and a crimson centre. Look out particularly for 'Sunningdale Variegated' which has large, pointed leaves of green marked with yellow and cream and flowers of white flushed pink.

Elephant's Ears (Bergenia)
These plants will also do well in shade. See page 162.

Marsh Marigold (Caltha palustris)
This attractive plant will grow well in moist soil in shade. See page 102.

Bugbane (Cimicifuga)
Tall, elegant plants with broad, ferny leaves and 'bottle-brush' flowers of white, yellow or cream, borne on wiry stems.

Bleeding Heart (Dicentra)
The common garden plant *Dicentra spectabilis* is perhaps the most attractive. It forms a hummock of attractive, delicate foliage topped by drooping sprays of white and red flowers. There are also white, pink and yellow forms.

Shooting Star (Dodecatheon meadia)
Forms a clump of primula-like leaves with pinky-mauve, pointed flowers with turned-back petals. It grows to about 15 inches (38 cm).

Hellebore (Helleborus)
The Christmas rose (*Helleborus niger*) and the lenten rose (*H. orientalis*) are amongst the best of plants for early spring. They all have handsome, glossy leaves and sculptured flowers of green, white and purple, often with superb markings inside.

Day Lily (Hemerocallis)
Very easy plants with bright green, arching leaves and lily-like flowers of bright yellow, pink, orange or buff. They reach between 2 and 4 feet (60–120 cm).

Coral Flower (Heuchera)
Clump-forming plants with rounded, hairy leaves, some attractively tinted and mottled grey. They produce dainty spires of flowers of cream, white or pink, mostly in early summer.

Below: Plantain Lily (*Hosta fortunei hyacinthiaia*)
Right: *Phlox paniculata* 'Tenor'
Bottom: *Senecio greyi*

Plantain Lily (Hosta)
There are dozens of superb hostas, all worth growing in a shady spot. They form clumps of beautiful foliage with generally heart-shaped leaves of green, yellow, bluish or variegated. The flowers arise mostly in summer and are generally white or lilac. They come in a wide variety of heights, depending on variety.

Houttuynia cordata
This will grow well in any moist soil. See page 102.

Dead-nettle (Lamium maculatum)
Excellent plants for covering a lot of ground quickly. They can become invasive but are easily chopped out with a spade. They have attractive foliage and masses of white or pink flowers in spring. Recommended are 'Aureum', which has yellow foliage, the green and silver 'Beacon Silver' and the green and white-leafed 'Shell-Pink' which also has pink flowers.

Golden Rays (Ligularia)
Striking plants up to 5 feet (150 cm) tall with large, rounded leaves of green or bronze-purple. They have tall heads of orange or yellow daisies in summer. They are, unfortunately, very prone to slug damage.

Purple Loosestrife (Lythrum)
Tall plants growing to about 4 feet (120 cm), with swaying heads of pinkish-purple in late summer.

Himalayan Poppies (Meconopsis)
Marvellous flowers of blue, yellow or white according to species, but most need an acid soil. Many forms have superb foliage often covered in reddish hairs. The easiest is the Welsh poppy (*Meconopsis cambrica*) which does well in any garden soil and has ferny green foliage and bright yellow flowers. It is a quick coloniser so may need some controlling. But if you are lucky and have an acid soil, don't miss *M. betonicifolia*, which bears flowers of the most exquisite blue with yellow stamens.

Solomon's Seal (Polygonatum hybridum)
A graceful plant growing to about 3 feet (90 cm), with arching stems bearing pendulous white flowers. 'Variegatum' is a good variegated form.

Knotweed (Polygonum)
A large family of superb ground-coverers, some growing to 4 feet (120 cm) tall though most grow to 1 to 2 feet (30–60 cm). They spread rapidly and some can become a nuisance. They carry spikes of flower in profusion over a long period in summer and autumn. One of the best is *Polygonum affine* 'Superbum', which has deep pink flowers.

Primula
Another large family with some real gems in it. The Candelabra group of primulas have flowers arranged in whorls up their stems, while the Himalayan cowslip (*Primula florindae*) carries drooping bells of soft yellow for a very long period. The drumstick primula (*P. denticulata*) has round heads of soft lavender or white.

Lungwort (Pulmonaria)
There are many varieties, all of which make good ground cover for the middle of the border. They have lance-shaped, often spotted leaves and tubular flowers of pink, blue or white in early spring.

Rhubarb (Rheum)
If you have a lot of room, grow the giant *Rheum palmatum* 'Atrosanguineum', which has enormous reddish leaves and 6-foot (180 cm) tall flower stems. In small gardens, stick to 'Ace of Hearts' which is much smaller but with similar dark leaves and 4-foot (120 cm) spikes of dainty pink flowers.

Many spring-flowering bulbs will do well in borders that are shaded by trees all summer, because, of course, the bulbs will flower well before the trees are in leaf. Many are woodland plants by nature in any case. Most autumn-flowerers will relish the shady conditions too.

Summer bedding plants are not so happy in these conditions, though I would certainly grow love-in-a-mist (*Nigella damascena*), *Phacelia campanularia*, flax (*Linum*), lobelia, busy-Lizzie (*Impatiens*), nasturtium and lavatera. All these, of course, can be raised from seed.

The dry, shady border
Not such a happy situation and my list will, I'm afraid, be a lot shorter. Do as much as you can to alleviate the conditions by pruning trees judiciously if you can and certainly by

Right: Guelder Rose (*Viburnum opulus* 'Sterile'
Below: Golden Marguerite (*Athemis tinctoria* 'Wargrave'
Bottom: Masterwort (*Astrantia major*)

improving the soil regularly with as much organic matter as you can lay your hands on. Under trees, raising the soil a little can help, bringing your plants above the root-range of the trees. But don't overdo it or the trees may suffer.

Shrubs for dry shade

Snowy Mespilus (Amelanchier lamarckii)
This can be grown as a shrub as well as a tree and it does well in dry shade, provided the soil is acid. See page 143.

Barberry (Berberis)
These really are the most accommodating of shrubs. Most will do well in this situation. See page 157.

Spindle (Euonymus)
All the evergreen types will do well in dry shade and cover quite a bit of ground. The light-coloured, variegated varieties

like *Euonymus fortunei* 'Emerald Gaiety' will brighten up a dark spot. See page 159.

Ivy (Hedera)
The best ivies in this situation are *Hedera colchica* and *H. hibernica*. See page 169.

Holly (Ilex)
The hollies are excellent plants for this difficult situation. There are several brightly variegated forms which will brighten things up a lot. If you want berries for Christmas, go for *Ilex aquifolium* 'J.C. Van Thol', and for a variegated form, use 'Golden King' or 'Silver Queen'.

Oregon Grape (Mahonia aquifolium)
One of the most reliable flowering shrubs in this position. They have glossy green leaves and bright yellow flowers in early spring, followed by blue-black berries. They tend to get a bit straggly so may want cutting back from time to time.

Pachysandra terminalis
A reliable ground-coverer with rosettes of green foliage and white flowers.

Stag's Horn Sumach (Rhus typhina)
A fine foliage plant with striking divided leaves and carrying large velvety brown cones in autumn. Very vivid red autumn colour.

Golden Elder (Sambucus nigra 'Aurea')
Another plant to brighten your darkness. See page 170.

Skimmia
Excellent everygreens for dry shade. See page 170.

Herbaceous perennials for dry shade
Bugle (Ajuga reptans)
There are several varieties available, with red, green, gold or purple foliage. All have blue flowers.

Lady's Mantle (Alchemilla mollis)
Will also do well in dry shade. See page 171.

Arum italicum 'Pictum'
Exotic leaves show in autumn and stand the hardest winter. In April the leaves stand up about 1 foot (30 cm), spear-shaped

and attractively veined white. There are vivid red berries in September.

Elephant's Ears (Bergenia)
These adaptable plants provide good ground cover but may flower a little less prolifically in dry shade. See page 162.

Siberian Bugloss (Brunnera macrophylla)
The common name makes this plant sound most unattractive, which is the complete reverse of the truth! It has beautiful, heart-shaped foliage, making good ground cover which, in spring, is topped by delicate sprays of forget-me-not type flowers.

Bowles 'Golden Grass' (Mileum effusum 'Aureum')
A small grass which brightens up a dark corner with golden, grass-like foliage and clusters of light brown flowers in June.

Bleeding Heart (Dicentra)
This will also do well in dry shade. See page 172.

Foxglove (Digitalis)
The hybrids of the common foxglove (*Digitalis purpurea*) come in a variety of colours and are easily raised from seed. They make tall, stately plants for the back of the border. These are strictly biennials though they may last a year or two. There are some perennial varieties including *D. ferruginea*, which grows to about 3 feet (90 cm) and has coppery yellow trumpets veined brown. *D. parviflora* has unusual bronze–brown flowers in July.

Barrenwort (Epimedium)
Low-growing, ground-cover perennials grown mainly for their attractive, heart-shaped brownish foliage. In March they bear tiny sprays of columbine-like flowers.

Spurge (Euphorbia)
Many spurges do well in dry shade. See page 165.

Cranesbill (Geranium)
Dry shade particularly suits *Geranium macrorrhizum* varieties which have aromatic leaves and good autumn colour. Flowers are in various shades of pink. See page 165.

Stinking Hellebore (Helleborus foetidus)
This hellebore does particularly well in dry shade. It is a smaller plant than most, with fresh green bells all winter and early spring. See also page 172.

Hypericum androseanum
The leaves of this medium-sized shrubby perennial have a reddish tinge and it bears yellow flowers followed by bronze berries which later turn black. It grows to about 2 feet (60 cm).

Dead-nettle (Lamium)
These ground-coverers will grow almost anywhere. See page 174.

Lily-turf (Liriope muscari)
A dwarf for the front of the border. In autumn, the clumps of grassy leaves carry violet-blue flowers like grape-hyacinths.

Lungwort (Pulmonaria)
Most pulmonarias will do well in dry shade.See page 175.

Piggy-back Plant (Tolmeia menziesii 'Variegata')
An attractive, low-growing ground-coverer with yellow-speckled, rounded leaves. It grows small plants on the top of the leaves which will root if pressed into the ground. Often grown as a house plant but perfectly hardy.

Labrador Violet (Viola labradorica)
An invasive but beautiful ground-coverer with small purple leaves and masses of light purple flowers.

Waldsteinia ternata
A creeping evergreen with glossy, lobed leaves and sprays of yellow flowers in spring.

Annual bedding does not do well in dry shade but some of the smaller early-spring flowering bulbs like snowdrops and bluebells are certainly worth a try. Autumn-flowering crocus and hardy cyclamen are also worth trying.

FRUIT AND VEGETABLES

Setting up a vegetable plot
In small modern gardens, a vegetable plot is really a luxury. In our garden in Birmingham, we had to make do with growing vegetables in the borders with the flowers and restricting our fruit mainly to the fences. Mind you, there's nothing wrong with that. In fact, vegetables can be quite attractive, especially those that take up least space, like the salads. And I reckon they'll be the ones you'll most want to grow.

Fruit trees can be almost as handsome as trees bred especially for their blossom. Apples, pears, plums, cherries, peaches, apricots and nectarines can all be grown in the shape of a fan on the fence, all have marvellous blossom in the spring and all have the added beauty of fruit to look at and to eat too. Who could ask for more?

What to grow
First of all, decide what is sensible to grow in the space available. There's absolutely no point in growing maincrop potatoes, for example, if space is limited. The farmer can do them just as cheaply and of equal quality to yours. Peas are probably even better frozen than home-grown (now *there's* a terrible thing for a gardener to admit!), because the processors pick them at just the right time, when they're at their sweetest. They take up a lot of space, so is it worth bothering?

Mind you, most vegetables, and especially the salads, are much, much better picked fresh from the garden. By the time they've been harvested, stood in the wholesale market, then in the shop and finally in your car getting them home, they're limp and tasteless. So, the first rule is to grow what is much better picked absolutely fresh. I would include in that all the salads, beans of every description, marrows and courgettes, spinach and sweet-corn.

Then look to grow what's most expensive or impossible to buy. I wouldn't be without my annual feast of globe artichokes, for example, but you can't find them in many greengrocers at a price you can afford!

Deep-bed growing
If you're short of space, then a deep-bed is what you want.

I've found that with this method you can increase the yield of vegetables per square yard by *at least* a hundred per cent and with some crops you can triple it! What's more it's easier to weed and cultivate and a productive deep-bed looks very attractive indeed from the kitchen window.

It's really a very simple system, based on the practice of growing everything in 4-foot (120 cm) wide beds rather than in conventional rows. All the work is done from the side-paths, just by reaching in as far as the middle, so you never actually tread on the beds.

It's pretty obvious that just by doing away with the access paths in between each row of vegetables, you can save yourself a lot of space. Of course, the vegetables still need room to grow, but they can be put much closer together. Lettuces are a good example. If you grow them in a block of, say, six rows with 8 inches (20 cm) between each plant, you'll take up 4 ft × 4 ft (120 cm × 120 cm) of space. If you leave a 1-foot (30 cm) path between each row on the conventional method, you'll take up 6 ft × 4 ft (180 cm × 120 cm). Put it another way; by the traditional row method you'd get 28 lettuces out of a 4 ft × 4 ft (120 cm × 120 cm) space, while by using the bed method, you'd get 42.

That would work if you cultivated the soil by single-digging only, but if you double-dig (see pages 41–43) there's a bonus. By extending the depth of the root-zone, you bring more soil area into use. If you improve the lower levels of the soil with organic matter to make it desirable for root growth, you extend the area they have from which to draw nutrients and water. That means they'll spread out less nearer the surface so you can space the vegetables a little closer. So doing it this way, you can get even more out of the restricted space than ever you thought possible.

And there's one other great advantage with double-digging. You'll raise the surface of the bed by about 6 inches (15 cm) above the rest of the garden. That means that drainage will be greatly improved so the soil will be drier and warmer and easier to work. And that's certainly the answer if your soil is heavy.

Mind you, there is a price to pay. Naturally, when you're growing as intensively as this, it's necessary to put back into the soil as much, or even a little more, than you take out. But that cost, believe me, is a fraction of the money you'll save by growing your own.

There are one or two crops that are not worth growing by

this method. Brussels sprouts, for example, need a lot of room whichever way you grow them. I've experimented with them closer than 2 feet (60 cm) apart and, though the plants grow well enough, the sprouts are too small to be worthwhile. They need that extra light, so there's no point in skimping on space.

Digging the bed

Start by marking out a 4-foot (120 cm) width with a couple of garden lines. Leave yourself at least 1 foot (30 cm) from the fence and between beds or you'll not get your bottom in the space when you bend down! If you find that reaching into the centre of a 4-foot (120 cm) wide bed is uncomfortable, there's no reason at all why you shouldn't make it a bit narrower.

If space is very restricted, it's a good idea to edge the beds with boards to keep the soil in. They look a lot neater that way too, though it's not absolutely necessary.

Deep beds are raised above the surrounding soil. They can be edged with boards to make them neater.

Then, if you have enough energy and enthusiasm to go the whole hog, double-dig the 4-foot (120 cm) strip, digging in plenty of manure, spent mushroom compost or peat. As I've suggested in my description of double-digging, it's necessary to work the organic matter through all levels of the soil, not just in the bottom trench, and I like to put a layer on the top too.

There's no need for extra soil to raise the beds; you'll find that the breaking up of the subsoil and the extra organic matter will do the trick.

You'll be pleased to hear that the hard work of double-digging need only be repeated once every five or six years depending on the soil. After the initial effort, you single-dig at the end of each season, but don't neglect the organic matter each year.

You'll read, by the way, that you should never use manure on land that is to be used for growing root crops because it makes them fork. Well I've certainly never found this to be true, provided the manure is well-rotted, so I would use it whatever you're growing. The same goes for spent mushroom compost, garden compost and peat.

Neither is there any need to bother with the complicated rotation plans that many traditional veg growers use. On a small scale like this, it will do nothing to avoid pests and diseases and, though you may deplete the soil of some essential nutrients, you'll be putting plenty back every year anyway. Just sow or plant wherever there's a convenient space.

Make shallow drills by resting the edge of the planting board on the soil and working it backwards and forwards.

Sowing and planting

I use a planting board for all sowing and planting. It's simply a length of wood with saw-cuts at 3-inch (7.5 cm) intervals along it. This not only gives you a reference for spacing, but it can be used instead of a line to give you a straight line.

If you're sowing small seeds, put the planting board across the bed in the right position, turn it on edge and just work it backwards and forwards so that it makes a shallow dent in the soil. Sow the seed thinly in the drill and then cover it by dragging the back of the rake gently down the middle of the drill. Tap it down gently with the back of the rake, mark each end with a label and Bob's your uncle. If the soil is dry when you come to sow, make the drill and run a little water into it from a can *before* you sow – never afterwards. Cover the drill with dry soil.

Large seeds need a slightly deeper drill, but don't go over the top. More seeds fail because they're sown too deeply than anything else, so never put them deeper than twice the depth of the seed itself, if you see what I mean. So broad beans should go about 1 inch (2.5 cm) deep. Make the drill with a stick, first anchoring your planting board into position with a couple of short canes behind it.

This is the way to use the board for planting as well, so you have a good indicator for the spacing and the straight line too.

Always plant in blocks rather than rows, staggering the plants to save further on space.

Before you sow or plant anything, sprinkle a bit of general fertiliser over the area and rake it in. Use about 3 to 4 handfuls of Growmore or blood, fish and bonemeal over every yard run of bed.

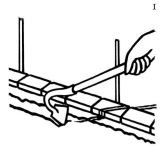

1. Deeper drills are made with a draw hoe, using the edge of the planting board as a guide.
2. By planting or sowing in blocks rather than in rows, you can save a great deal of space.
3. A simple wooden bridge is not difficult to make and will save miles of walking, especially if the bed is long.

1

If your deep-bed is any length at all, you'll find that to avoid treading on the soil you'll walk miles! When sowing or planting, you can only do half a row from one side-path and then you have to walk round to get at the other half. If the bed is short, that's no problem but, if it's long, you'll be cursing my name before very long! So I should advise you to build yourself a wooden bridge. It's not difficult to make out of scrap timber and, if you fix a length of rope to the top, you'll find it quite easy to move about. I use mine all the time and it saves miles of walking.

Deep-bed spacings

2

Beetroot – 3 inches (7.5 cm)
Broad beans – 9 inches (23 cm)
Spring cabbage – 6 in × 12 in (15 cm × 30 cm)
Summer cabbage – 12 inches (30 cm)
Winter cabbage – 18 inches (45 cm)
Chinese cabbage – 10 inches (25 cm)
Peppers – 18 inches (45 cm)
Carrots – 6 inches (15 cm)
Summer cauliflower – 18 inches (45 cm)
Autumn and winter cauliflower – 24 inches (60 cm)
Self-blanching celery – 9 inches (23 cm)
Ridge cucumber – 24 inches (60 cm)
French beans – 18 inches (45 cm)
Leeks – 16 inches (15 cm)
Lettuce – 6 to 9 inches (15–23 cm) (depending on variety)
Marrow and courgette – 24 inches (60 cm)
Onion – 6 inches (15 cm)
Parsnip – 6 inches (15 cm)
Early potatoes – 9 inches (23 cm)
Shallot – 6 inches (15 cm)
Spinach – 6 inches (15 cm)
Swede – 12 inches (30 cm)
Sweet-corn – 18 inches (45 cm)
Bush tomatoes – 18 inches (45 cm)

3

Turnip – 6 inches (15 cm)
Radish and salad onions should be sown in a 4-inch (10 cm) wide band and scattered thinly. They need no thinning.

Vegetables in the borders

If, like us, you don't even have room for a small deep-bed, you'll have to resort to growing a few veg in the borders. They do, in fact mix in very well. Ideally, think ahead a little when it comes to planning the ornamental plantings and leave the odd space here and there. In this case, it would look quite wrong to sow or plant in long, straight rows. Here you grow in clumps so, if you are raising the vegetables from seed, sow very short rows in patches exactly as advised for hardy annuals (see page 138).

Climbing vegetables, like beans, peas, marrows and cucumbers, can be grown against the wires or trellis fixed to the fences, where they'll fit in very well and add an unusual touch of interest as well as a useful crop.

Some plants are particularly decorative and better suited to the border than the deep-bed. I grow all my globe artichokes, in the borders, for example, where they provide exotic grey foliage with dramatic great thistle-like leaves up to 4 feet (120 cm) tall.

On a smaller scale, a clump of beetroot looks very attractive, especially planted in conjunction with grey foliage or white flowers. The bright-red-leafed rhubarb chard looks even better. And, of course, a clump of rhubarb itself makes an excellent foliage effect.

One of the great advantages with growing vegetables mixed in with the flowers in this way is that they are much less likely to suffer from pests or diseases. Often insects home in on their victims by sight and the camouflage provided by surrounding ornamental plants has been shown to help hide the vegetables away. The wide diversity of planting also helps to mask characteristic scents which could give insects a clue, and it attracts the insect enemies of the pests, which themselves make for a very effective means of control.

Growing herbs

Of course, herbs can also be grown in the borders to good effect. This is an essential ingredient of a *real* cottage garden, I suppose, and certainly it's the best way to grow the taller varieties like lovage and angelica. But it's nice to have a small area devoted to herbs for use in the kitchen somewhere near the back door where they're readily available. In our Birmingham garden, we included a small patch of mixed herbs right under the kitchen window. You simply can't get them fresher than that!

But it's important to get to know a little about the way the plants grow and to stick to those that aren't going to take over. Where room is limited, I would suggest that it's best to grow only those that are in constant use in the kitchen. Our own list was necessarily limited.

Perhaps the most popular of all herbs is mint, and that's where the problems start. This is a really invasive plant with underground runners that will very quickly take over the whole garden if you're not careful. It's often suggested that to prevent it getting out of hand it should be grown in a bucket sunk into the ground in the herb garden. My own experience is that even that is risky. You only need one shoot to pop over the top of the bucket and root into the soil (which it will do very readily indeed), and it's away. So my suggestion would be to grow it in a container on the patio. There it can never do any harm and it'll make a nice-looking pot too.

Parsley is widely used but difficult to grow from seed. Either germinate it on the windowsill and plant it out later or buy the plants from the garden centre. It makes a very good edging to the bed.

Chives also make an attractive edging and a very useful culinary herb too. But you don't need to buy enough plants to edge the whole bed. Buy one, plant it out as a clump and then split it up the following year. You'll have more than enough and some to give away too!

Garlic is a matter of opinion. I wouldn't be without it, but some more sociable folk would never eat it! If you do grow it, buy a bulb from the greengrocer or the seed merchant and split it up into individual cloves. These are planted in March in the sunniest spot in the garden.

Sage and thyme are best bought as plants. There are several coloured varieties of both, which will brighten up an uninteresting corner. The variegated varieties are just as good in the kitchen as the plain ones.

One other herb that no good cook should be without is bay. You can buy plants from the garden centre but do bear in mind that it's tender and will suffer in a hard winter. So unless you live in a favoured spot, grow it in a tub and bring it inside for the winter.

Growing fruit

Fruit-growing in small gardens used to be difficult. Trees like apples, pears, plums and cherries grew to such enormous dimensions that most modern gardens would certainly only have room for one. That, of course, could also mean problems of pollination, because most fruit needs another variety to ensure that the fruits set. Today, I'm pleased to report, no such problems exist.

First of all, several types of fruit can now be grown on

'dwarfing rootstocks'. This is a technique where the variety is grafted onto a special set of roots which will control the vigour of the tree. So even monsters like the cooking apple 'Bramley's Seedling', which is so vigorous on its own roots it would take up the whole of a small garden, can now be reduced to a tree no bigger than 8 or 10 feet (2.5–3 m).

Training methods have also undergone changes, so very simple pruning methods will keep trees down to a manageable size too. What's more, they enable you to grow trees that look really attractive.

Tree fruit

In order to keep trees fruitful and within bounds, they need to be pruned every year. And I know it's that which puts most new gardeners off growing them. The instructions for pruning are generally so complicated they become totally incomprehensible. If it's any consolation, I've never understood them either!

Cordon apples are grown at an angle and take up very little space.

In fact, if you stick to growing small, trained trees, the method is so simple you'll wonder why you ever worried. To grow apples and pears, you need to learn one method which will do for everything, so once you know how to prune a cordon, you've got the whole story. I have to admit that fan-trained peaches, apricots and nectarines do get a bit complicated so I would suggest you stick, in the first instance, to apples, pears, plums and cherries and graduate to the more difficult stuff when you've mastered those.

Cordons are single-stemmed trees, generally grown at an angle of 45 degrees and trained onto wires either free-standing or fixed to the fence. They're planted $2\frac{1}{2}$ feet (75 cm) apart. This is a method suitable for apples and pears in the main though I have seen plums grown as cordons too.

Buy one or two-year-old plants from a fruit specialist. They'll consist of a strong main stem and perhaps, though not necessarily, a few side-branches. Plant them $2\frac{1}{2}$ feet (75 cm) apart against a cane tied at a 45 degree angle to the fence or wire structure. Immediately after planting, prune the main stem back, cutting off about a third of its length. When you prune, cut back cleanly, just above a bud. Cut the side-branches back to leave them 2 inches (5 cm) long.

That's all the pruning you do in the winter. Next August, the side-shoots you pruned in the winter will have grown out. Cut back all of the new growth to leave little shoots 1 inch (2.5 cm) long. If new side-shoots have grown out from the

A small herb garden can make a very attractive feature, but make sure you choose carefully to avoid the really rampant growers. We planted out culinary herbs right outside the kitchen window where they scented the kitchen and were in easy reach of the back door.

We planted some espalier apples in our small garden where space was too limited to grow them as free-standing trees.

main stem, cut them back to 2 inches (5 cm). And that's it! Remember, new side-shoots coming from the main stem cut to 2 inches (5 cm) and any coming from those to 1 inch (2.5 cm).

Fans are also grown against a fence in, believe it or not, the shape of a fan. You can buy trees already trained so there's no need to worry about the initial formation of the shape. Before planting, fix 8-foot (20 cm) canes to the wires so that the shoots can be tied in to those instead of directly onto the wires, which will chafe.

Plant these 12 feet (3.5 m) apart. To prune them, look at each branch separately and treat it just as if it was a cordon.

Espaliers are much the same as fans except that the branches are trained out horizontally, one above the other, to form a series of 'tiers'. This shape is used mainly for apples and pears, and again, you can buy them already trained.

Once more, take each branch separately and treat it like a cordon.

Free-standing trees can be kept down to size by a method known as 'festooning', where branches are bent down and tied onto the main stem or the branch below.

Plant one or two-year-old trees not less than 6 feet (18 cm) apart. Then pull the main stem carefully into an arc and tie it to the trunk at the bottom. If there are other strong branches, these can be treated in the same way.

In August, you'll find that side-shoots have grown out all along the curved stem. Then, select about four more branches for tying down in the same way and treat the rest like cordons. Cut new shoots arising from the main stem back to 2 inches (5 cm) and any coming from them to 1 inch (2.5 cm). Repeat that every August and you'll get an interesting shape and a small, very fruitful tree.

Bear in mind that no apple or pear will set a full crop of fruit without being pollinated, so two trees are needed and they should be different varieties that flower at the same time. The fruit-grower you buy the trees from will certainly be able to advise.

Plums are no more difficult. You can grow a small festooned tree, pruning it in just the same way as described for apples, or you can fan train it against the fence.

It's essential to buy a self-pollinating variety, so I would advise you to stick with 'Victoria', which is just about the best dessert plum there is anyway. It's also important to buy a tree that has been grafted onto a dwarfing rootstock, so ask for 'Victoria' on 'Pixy', which will keep the tree quite small.

For fans, it's best to start out with a ready-trained tree. Plant it against a south or west-facing fence if you can, though they will also do quite well elsewhere. You'll need some horizontal wires fixed to the posts again and you should tie to these a number of 8-foot (2.5 m) canes in the shape you require. Then tie the shoots of the tree to the canes.

The only pruning that's necessary is to pinch out the growing tips of shoots you *don't* want in the summer as soon as they've made about six leaves. Any shoots that are overcrowded or have just outgrown their space should be treated like this. Then, as soon as the fruit has been picked, cut those shoots you've pinched back again, this time to leave three buds.

Sweet cherries can be treated in the same way. Again, a self-pollinating variety is essential and there's only one – 'Stella' – so that solves that little problem! This time, buy it grafted onto the rootstock 'Colt', but since this is only semi-dwarfing, you'll be well advised to grow the tree as a fan, where you can control the growth. Prune in the same way as a plum.

Espaliers can be grown to the top of the fence, with several 'tiers' spaced about 1 foot (30 cm) apart. They are very productive and make a bright show of blossom and fruit.

Soft fruit

Soft fruit – strawberries, raspberries, gooseberries, black and red currants – are invaluable, so try to find a space for a few if you can.

Blackcurrants take up quite a bit of space but are very rewarding. Choose a modern variety like 'Ben More' or 'Malling Jet', which are very heavy cropping. If you're growing more than one bush, plant them at least 5 feet

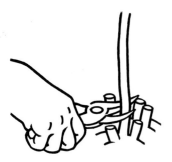

Blackcurrants should be pruned right down to the ground immediately after planting.

(150 cm) apart. They're very heavy feeders and don't like competition. Plant the bushes a little deeper than they grew on the nursery, and afterwards cut all the shoots right back to 1 inch (2.5 cm) above the ground. This will mean that you lose the first year's fruit, but you'll build yourself a strong bush with new growth coming right from the bottom. Every year, the wood that has fruited should be cut out in this way.

Redcurrants and gooseberries are treated alike, but a bit differently to blackcurrants. They are grown on a 'leg', so plant them with the top of the pot at soil level and prune the shoots back by no more than half. Again, plant 5 feet (150 cm) apart. The best gooseberries are either 'Jubilee' or 'Invicta' and the favourite redcurrant is 'Red Lake'.

Raspberries need a post and wire support, or again, wires on the fence-posts. Choose a variety like 'Glen Clova' or 'Malling Jewel' and plant about 18 inches (45 cm) apart. Again, the shoots should be cut right back to leave just a few inches to encourage shoots to come from the base. New canes will arise from the bottom and these should be tied onto the wires, directly this time, not on canes, spacing them about 4 inches (10 cm) apart along the wires. They'll provide the crop for the following year and should be cut right out after fruiting, to leave space to tie in the new canes. Autumn-fruiting varieties like 'Malling Joy' need no support. Plant them in the same way and cut them right down hard every February. They'll grow up to give you a crop the same year.

Strawberries are the quickest to produce a crop. Ideally, buy new plants in September and you'll get your first picking the following June. If you have room, buy a few varieties to give a longer succession of picking. 'Tamella' is a good early, followed by 'Hapil' and finally the autumn-fruiting 'Aromel'. Plant them in beds with three rows 18 inches (45 cm) apart and 2 feet (60 cm) between plants. When you plant, make sure that the 'crown' of the plant, where the leaves join the roots, is exactly at soil level.

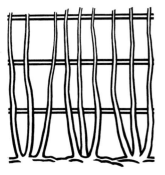

Raspberries must be trained against a post and wire structure or on the fence.

INDEX

Page numbers in *italic* refer to the illustrations